Little R
of
Grammar Made Easy

Little Red Book
of
Grammar Made Easy

Terry O'Brien

RUPA

Published by
Rupa Publications India Pvt. Ltd 2011
7/16, Ansari Road, Daryaganj
New Delhi 110002

Sales centres:
Allahabad Bengaluru Chennai
Hyderabad Jaipur Kathmandu
Kolkata Mumbai

ISBN: 978-81-291-1805-9

Fourth impression 2014

10 9 8 7 6 5 4

The moral right of the author has been asserted.

Typeset by Innovative Processors, Delhi

Printed at Shree Maitrey Printech Pvt. Ltd., Noida

*I dedicate this book to late Prof. A.P. O'Brien,
my father, friend, guide and mentor, who
inspired me to the canon of excellence:
re-imagining what's essential*

PREFACE

This book is an introduction to Standard English. The book gives the suiting of language to purpose. It spells out the rules of grammar. And it gives and lays down what is acceptable usage. This is for daily users of English with new models and examples. The aim is to increase the reader's skills in handling language.

- **Standard English** is the variety of English taught in the educational systems of the English-speaking world. It is also taught to students in those parts of the world where English is the second language. Spoken and written English with differences of vocabulary, accent and idiom peculiar to different parts of the world- enables the understanding of the widest audience. Standard English is the written English of the business letter, report writing, novels, newspapers, and the spoken English of the job interview and the television documentary. It is language used when language needs a certain degree of formality.

- **English in the world** Sometimes a language is so far removed from standard English in the words and expressions used, that it confuses many. It is in developing countries that the spoken form is achieving an identity of its own. Indian English, has acquired words from other native languages (*lakh*= a sum of money, *goonda*= a hooligan. New phrases (*gunnysack*=sack), mixes Indian and English expressions (newspaper *wallah*- a man who sells newspapers and has inventive lines in insults and politenesses. This form of English is achieving respectability that makes British English seem somewhat old-fashioned and out of touch. This is the 'living' language.

- **Modern trends** mirror the enormous social and political changes which have taken place over the century. This is 'informality' par excellence. Politicians, journalists and broadcasters now use a language which is more informal and accessible than used. Earlier 'good' English was rather high-flown and was artificial in style and spoken with an exaggerated 'Public School' accent. Today we talk in a kind of verbal shorthand, making use of colloquial expressions. "Yes we can" gave America its first Afro-American President.

- **Colloquial language** (conversational) or slang is caused by the fluidity of language-*boss*, *mob*, or *rock* (music) with the passage of times gain respectability. We use *great*/wonderful; *cool*/fashionable; *chill out*/calm down; *blow up*/lose one's temper and more. The margin between colloquial language and slang is rather thin. If a word is extreme or colorful we call it slang. Slang words are often short lived. They pass in and out fashion and trend. Money was *dough*, *bread* and *bucks*.

- **Accent** stems from the region and social class of our birth. RP or Received Pronunciation has lost its monopoly.

There is only one thing in the world that is permanent: change. So is it with the speed with which language seems to change. The correct use of language has no definite parameter. Usage is forever on the fast track of change. Then what about the strict Grammarian's dictum?

A person may kick a ball randomly and impress his folks with his playing skills. But most certainly he cannot play the game of football unless he knows the grammar of the game. So be it with language! But while knowing the rules, one may get lost in the labyrinth of definitions.

Beware. Enjoy the skills of language application and don't fall a victim to definitions. Look beyond. Then shall you develop '*response-ability*'. This book is an extremely simplified look at the nuances of English language.

PARTS OF SPEECH

The machinery of language can help us understand the various different sorts of words and how they function.

Some words have simple functions (for example describing or saying what happened) whereas others can be used for many different ones. Look at the word *round* in the following examples:

> A *round* building, the third *round* of the match; come *round* for a chat

In each case *round* is performing a different function (describing, naming, being part of an action). The technical term used to describe these functions are called '**parts of speech**'.

Nouns

A noun is a naming word from the Latin *nomen* (name).

It may name a specific person, creature, place or object (proper nouns):

> Ruskin Bond, Spot, New Delhi, the *Independent*.

It may name an individual belonging to a class of people, animals or things that can be directly seen, heard, touched or smelt (**common noun**):

> Doctor, dog, house, bicycle, water, smell.

It may be a quality, state of mind, attitude, idea or action that does not refer directly to the senses (**abstract noun**):

> Intelligence, happiness, laziness, democracy, philosophy, violence.

It may refer to a group of individual people or animals (**collective noun**):

> army, audience, flock, family, jury, majority.

Nouns are either singular – referring to one only:

> tree, woman, quality

Or plural – more than one:

> trees, women, qualities.

Pronouns

A pronoun stands in place of a noun: *she, we, it, everybody*.

Pronouns are a handy device for avoiding the repetition of nouns. Instead of writing:

> The car windshield has been broken. The car had been damaged in an accident.

We are able to write:

> The car windshield has been broken. It had been damaged in an accident.

Pronouns may be singular (*I, he, she, it*) or plural (*we, they*); the pronoun *you* may be singular or plural depending on whether it refers to one person or to several.

The most important categories of pronoun are:

a. personal e.g. I, me, mine; you, yours, he, him, his; ours;

b. **demonstrative** e.g. this, these, that, those (as in *This belonged to my father*);

   c. **interrogative** e.g. who, whose, which, what (as in *Who did that?*);
   d. **indefinite** e.g. anybody, none, no one, either, each;
   e. **relative** e.g. who, whose, what, whom, that;
   f. **reflexive** e.g. myself, ourselves, yourself, itself, himself.

Relative pronouns are so called because, as well as acting as pronouns, they relate or join groups of words.

Adjectives

An adjective describes a noun or pronoun:

   enthusiastic, sixth, tallest, invisible.

Adjectives are normally placed before the nouns they describe (*several large elephants*) but other positions are possible.

   The morning was *misty* and *cold*.

   The morning, *misty* and *cold*, depressed his spirits.

If adjectives are formed from proper nouns they have capital letters (the *Indian* way of life, the *Christian* religion).

It is a particular flexibility of English that words which are used as nouns may be used as adjectives (*alarm* clock, *police* van, *chicken* soup).

Comparison of adjectives

When comparing only two persons or things, use the *–er* form of the adjective:

   Rohan is *taller* than his sister.

Which is *newer*, this one or that one.

When the adjective has no *–er* form, and in some cases to avoid clumsiness, use *more*:

That puppy is *more active* than this one.

His painting is *more interesting* than hers.

When comparing three or more, use the *–est* form:

Rohit is the *tallest* of the three.

The *tiniest* kitten is the *prettiest*.

When the adjective has no *–est* form, use *most*:

He is by far the *most determined* of all.

This is by far the *most sensible* of your proposals.

Verbs

A verb expresses an action or state of being: *walk, made, fought, seems, existed.*

He *mended* the puncture, *smiled, mounted* his bicycle, and *rode* away

We *are* very sad because they *have suffered* so much.

The garden *had been neglected* and the house *was ruined*.

In the first sentence, the four verbs are functioning on their own.

In the other two examples, they need to be helped by the auxiliary verbs *to be* and *to have* in their various forms: *have, had been* and *was*.

Adverbs

Adverbs describe or enlarge the meaning of a verb, adjective or other adverb.

He called *loudly*.

There was a *very* faint reply.

He called *more* loudly.

When an adverb describes a verb, it usually indicates *how*, *when*, *where* or *why* the action of the verb is taking place.

Adverbs that indicate *how* are often formed from adjectives.

   a. Usually one adds –*ly*: slow> *slowly*; strong > *strongly*,

   b. Adjectives ending in –*ue* drop the –*e*: due>duly; true>truly.

   c. Adjectives ending in –*y* change to –*ily*: happy>*happily*; ready>*readily*; funny>*funnily*.

   d. Adjectives ending in –*ll* add –*y* full>*fully*; shrill>*shrilly*.

   e. Adjectives ending in –*ic* add –*ally*: drastic >*drastically*; sarcastic>*sarcastically*.

Some adverbs have the same form as adjectives:

     A *long* time (*adj.*), did you wait *long*? (adv)A *fast* train (*adj.*), the car went fast. (*adv*)

Some adverbs affect the whole sentence, not just the verb:

     The book, *then*, makes an important contribution to our knowledge of food.

The adverb *then* has a dual purpose: it enlarges the meaning of the verb *makes*, and it also expresses a relationship between the whole sentence and what has gone before: in this case *then* expresses the conclusion.

Other forms of relationships with what has gone before can also be expressed by adverbs, usually near the beginning of the sentence, e.g.: *however, nevertheless, incidentally, moreover, likewise, besides, therefor*e.

Prepositions

A preposition is a word that is placed before a noun or pronoun to link it to another part of the sentence or to the sentence as a whole. There are a large number of these, including: *at, in, to, by, from, with, through, round*:

> *On* the beach Rajesh gazed at the dolphin *in* amazement.

> You must walk round the wood, not *through* it.

> Nitin and Nikita arrived *during* the afternoon, not *after* lunch as expected.

The preposition can affect the sense of some verbs, e.g. agree *with /on/to*:

> We agree *with* you and *with* the action you have taken.

> We agree *on* what we should do next.

> Your brother will not agree *to* our suggestion: we must agree *to* differ.

The same word may be a preposition or an adverb:

> Wait *outside* the door. (*preposition*)

Wait *outside*. (*adverb*)

Many sentences naturally end with a preposition.

What a mess your bedroom is *in!*

The husband was easy to talk *to;* the wife impossible to communicate *with*.

What did you mend it *with*? I made it all *up*.

Nowadays this is acceptable, although in the past it was absolutely forbidden and writers used to *go* to great lengths to avoid it.

On the other hand, a preposition at the end of a clause or sentence can sometimes sound awkward, especially in a formal context:

This is the college I spent three happy years *at*.

This would be better re-worded:

This is the college *at* which I spent three happy years.

Conjunctions

A conjunction connects two words or groups of words:

Orange *and* White stripes; take it *or* leave it;

I went to bed early *because* I was tired.

It need not always be placed between the words being linked:

Because I was tired, I went to bed early.
Although he was injured, he went on playing.

It is possible for a word to be a conjunction in one sentence and have a different function in another:

Look *before* you leap. (*Conjunction*)

It has happened *before*. (*Adverb*)

We left *before* the end. (*Preposition*)

Interjections or exclamations

An interjection or exclamation is a word or remark expressing emotion, usually sudden:

Aha! So it was you! You didn't expect to be caught, *eh*?

Ouch! That hurt! You *horror*!

Alas, it was the dog that died!

Words with more than one function

English grammar is very flexible and there are many examples of words performing several functions. For example, the nouns *dog*, *bus*, *leg* and *school* can all be used as verbs:

I am going to *leg* it home.

It is sensible to *bus* the children to school.

The word *down* is an example of a multi-function word:

Put it *down*! (adverb)

Let's walk *down* the hill (preposition)

The pillows are filled with *down* (noun)

A *down* payment of Rs 1000. (adjective)

The workforce decided to *down* tools (verb)

Down, dog, *down*! (interjection)

Basic units of language

A sentence communicates a complete action, thought or feeling to the reader or listener:

> Rohan kicked the ball.
>
> Harish thought she was in the kitchen.
>
> You should consider the matter most carefully.
>
> We were sorry you couldn't come to the party.

It may contain a maximum of five elements:

> subject; verb; objects(s); complement; adverbial.

but the shortest possible complete sentence need only consist of noun or pronoun (subject) and verb:

> Terry ran. He ran.
>
> Susan was singing. We were sorry.

In what appear to be incomplete sentences, the noun may be implied, not stated, or it may refer to words that went before:

> Run! (*Run, Terry!*)
>
> Keep off the grass. (*You* keep off.)
>
> *Rohan*. (In answer to *Who kicked the ball?*)
>
> Yes. (In answer to previous question)

Subject

The person or thing that performs the action of the verb is known as the **subject** of the sentence – when in doubt ask the question *Who* or *What did this?*

The subject may be a noun, a pronoun, or a set of words:

> *She* did a cartwheel but *he* fell over.

> *The cars* were lined up on the street.

Sometimes, mainly in commands, the subject is not stated but is clearly implied:

> *Keep off that park.* (implied is the word *you*)

Sometimes the subject of the sentence is a form of the verb such as a verbal noun (noun formed from a verb ending in –*ing*), as in:

> *Skating* would be foolhardy.

> *Shopping* is easier on Thursdays.

or a group of words (phrase) beginning with the *to* form of the verb (infinitive) such as:

> *To delay too long* would be a risk.

Object

The object of the verb is the person or thing that receives the action of the verb. It may be a noun, a pronoun, or a set of words. It is not essential for a verb to have an object. Some verbs never take an object (e.g. *sleep*, *rise*): these are called **intransitive** verbs.

> He was sleeping. They are trying very hard.

If a verb has an object it is called a **transitive** verb:

> I hurt *my toe*. Do you like *the colour*?
> Try *cycling*.

Some verbs sometimes have an object:

The neighbours *were burning* old newspapers.
and at other times do not have an object:

The lamps *were burning* brightly.

There are two kinds of object:

Direct object – a word or set of words affected directly by the verb:

> We welcomed *him.*

> He asked *what we were* doing.

Indirect object – a word or set of words *to* or *for* which the action of the verb is performed.

> The shop sold *him* a defective printer.

> They sent *all their customers* an offer of a refund.

Complement

Instead of, or as well as, an object, some verbs are followed by what is called a complement to complete the sentence. This may refer to the subject or the object:

Subject complements – some verbs (e.g. *to become, taste, seem, appear, look*) express a state rather than an action, and the rest of the sentence refers back to the subject of the verb:

> The dog looked *ill.*

> The town *remained* tense.

Note the difference between:

> He *made* a pudding

and

He *made* an excellent cricketer.

Object complements – other verbs are followed by a word or group of words that complete the meaning of the verb by referring to its object:

They kept it a *secret*.

I thought them a *bit crude*.

Agreement of subject and verb

When the subject is singular the verb must be singular to 'agree' with it:

Ruby *is* at home and so *is* her sister.

She *hears* her brother shouting and *wonders* why.

The dog *was* lying on the ground on its side.

When the subject is plural, the verb must be plural too:

Ruby and her sister *are* at home.

They *hear* their students shouting and *wonder* why.

Take care, When using longer sentences which contain two or more clauses, we must take care to make the verb agree with its own subject:

The dog *sees* the chicks which *are* quietly feeding and *runs* towards them.

Johnny, whose friends *are* all staring at him, quickly *leaves* the class room.

Verbs and tenses

The tense of a verb is the form it takes to make it clear when an action takes place. We can de-scribe an event as taking place in the past, or as happening in the present while we write, or as occurring at some time in the future.

The verbs we use to tell of these events must be in the corresponding tense: past, present or future.

Past tenses	Present tenses	Future tenses
He kicked the ball	He kicks the ball	He will kick the ball
He has kicked the ball	He is kicking the ball	He will be kicking the ball
He has been kicking the ball	He does kick the ball	He will have been kicking the ball
He was kicking the ball	The ball is being kicked	He will have kicked the ball
He did kick the ball		
The ball was being kicked		
He had kicked the ball		
He had been kicking the ball		

In writing, the simple rule is to keep to the tense you begin with unless there is some good reason to change it. The verbs in the following passage are all in the same tense, describing a sequence of actions in the past:

Raj shouted. The figure instantly disappeared. Raj moved cautiously forward. A spider's brushed against his forehead, startling him.

Finite and non-finite verb forms

The form of the verb that has a subject and a tense is called finite:

Everyone *uses* computers.

He *surfed* the net. They *ate* a burger.

A verb is in a **non-finite** form when it does not have a subject or does not form a whole tense, in which case it is either an **infinitive** form or a form of **participle**:

Infinite

It's easy to *understand*.

To *surf* the net you need to *get* on line.

The infinitive need not be a '*to*' form. If it follows a verb such as *can, could, would, should, must, may, might, shall* or *will*:

You might *eat* a pizza this evening.

You must *get up* early tomorrow.

Participle

Participles are of two kinds:	
a	'-ing' words, such as *running*, *walking*, *shopping*, which may appear with different functions in the sentence:
	Running is good exercise. (verbal noun)
	People were *running* from the building. (part of a tense)
	They fought a *running* battle. (adjective)
b	'-ed' forms (or –d, -t, -en, -n, etc. The '-ed' form is a verb form that is sometimes part of a tense:
	He has *complained*. I had not *kept* fit.
	Have you *chosen*?
	or it may be used as an adjective:
	burnt toast, *sworn* enemies, etc.

Active and passive verbs

A verb is active when the subject performs the action:

> He *misled* you.
> The company *built* the amplitheatre.
> The crew *launched* the life-boat.

It is passive when the subject 'suffers' the action:

> He was *misled* by you.
> The ampletheatrestadium was *built* by the company.
> The life-boat was *launched* by the crew.

Phrases

A phrase is a set of words containing a single idea that does not contain a finite verb. It has the same function in a sentence as a noun or pronoun, adjective or adverb.

Type of phrase	
His *former friends* helped him.	Noun
Do you know *his time* of *arrival*?	Noun
None of the students failed.	pronoun
The paper, *because of the* strike, will not be published	adverbial
The Maharaja, *arrogant as ever*, emerged from his BMW	adverbial
The tower, *now fallen into disrepair*, was demolished.	adjectival

A phrase may contain a non-finite '-ing' or 'to' form of the verb

Walking fast is an excellent exercise.

The people *hurrying from the field* were panic-stricken.

I heard his radio *playing western music*.

We decided to *run round the garden*.

or it may be used with an *–ed* form as in:

He woke up *refreshed by his sleep*.

Clauses

A clause is a set of words that contains a finite verb. If it makes sense on its own it is called a main clause: *He was angry* and he slapped the man.

If a clause does not make sense on its own it is called a subordinate clause. Like phrases, subordinate clauses perform different functions in the sentence:

Type of clause	
What he said surprised everyone	noun-subject
She regretted *that she had lost her temper*	noun-object
Forgetting that his keys were inside, he shut the door	adjectival
The tower, *which was falling down*, has been demolished	adjectival
The Prime Minister, *who was in Germany*, made a speech	adjectival
I was only nine *when my parents parted ways*	adverbial-when
I haven't a clue *where I have put it*	adverbial-where
He slammed the door *because he was angry*	adverbial-why
They played as *they had never played before*	adverbial-how

Punctuation

When we speak, we use various speech patterns, especially intonation and stress patterns make our meaning clear to the listener. We raise and lower our voices, pause for longer or shorter intervals, speak more quickly or more slowly, more loudly or more softly, and emphasize certain words and not others. We also help to make our meaning clear with body language – facial expressions, gestures and body movements and even eye contact.

However, when we write, we have only a set of punctuation marks to represent these speech patterns and body language. Used correctly, these rules give clarity to what we write clear to the reader.

Full stop (.)

The full stop is used to end a sentence and so separates one sentence from another.

> Dhoni is a fine cricketer. He often scores a century in one-day matches. He is also a very good wicket keeper.

> Listen, you cannot go yet. You must stay here until they tell you can leave.

It is also used in incomplete sentences such as :

> Fine, thank you (answer to a query about someone's health)

> No, certainly not. (answer to the question ' Will you do it ?)

Its second important use is to mark certain abbreviated words:

i.e. (Latin *id est* = that is, followed by an explanation of what has gone before)

e.g. (Latin *exempli gratia* = for example)

etc. (Latin *et cetera* + and so on, and the others) but it is no longer necessary in NB (Latin *nota bene*) or PS (*post scriptum*).

It is used in some abbreviated titles

Prof. *A.P. O'Brien*

It is not normally the practice to use a full point if the last letter of the abbreviation is the same as the last letter of the full form lf the word :

Mr, Mrs, Ms, Dr, St (street and saint), 6th, etc.

nor is it necessary to use it with academic degrees such as MA or BSc or with honours, or other titles such as MP.

It is optional to use full points in :

a.m. and p.m. (Latin ante and post meridiem)

A.D. *(anno domini) and B.C.* (before Christ)

R.S.V.P.(repondez s'il vous plait = Please reply).

Most letters made from initial letter such as BBC, ITV, MP, and UNICEF are spelt without them.

The full point is indeed as a decimal point in units of money (Rs 20.40) and percentages (1.5 percent), and is found in expressions of time to separate hours from minutes (14.25).

Question mark (?)

The question mark is needed at the end of a sentence that poses a question:

Who was that at the gate?

Even though a question may be worded as a statement :

You don't really believe that?

It is also needed at the end of a quoted question:

'Who was that on the telephone?' he asked.

At the end of a sentence, the question mark has the force of a full stop and is followed by a capital letter. Do not use a question mark *and* a full stop.

A question mark is not used at the end of a reported or implied (as distinct from a direct) question :

> He asked who was at the gate.

> I'd like to know whether or not you'll be coming.

Exclamation mark (!)

The exclamation mark is used instead of a full stop at anger, sustrain or enthusian end of a sentence expressing strong feelings, such as surprise, anger or enthusiasm.

> Put that glass down at once!

> What a splendid idea!

It allows the writer to choose between a mild expression of feeling :

> I never dreamt he would be so foolish. Please listen.

and a stronger one:

> I never dreamt he would be so foolish! Please listen!

You also use it after single words, or phrases (greeting, expletives, warnings, commands, cries for help, insults, etc.) which have an exclamatory nature:

> Oh! Good heavens! You idiot! Look out! What a pity!

> Hello! Hi! Cheers! Help! Hey!

It is not a rule that such expressions have to be followed by an exclamation mark; you have to decide whether the context calls for special strength. Note the difference between

> Hello there! Can you hear me?
>
> Good heavens! That's incredible!

and

> Hello, how are you?
>
> Good heavens, that was ages ago.

Comma (,)

The comma separates words, phrases or clauses when the sense demands a slight pause. There are few rules for it. The most common error, apart from using a comma when a full stop is essential, is over-use in a way that interrupts the flow of a sentence.

The best policy is to use a comma only when it contributes something to the sense.

Creating lists

Commas are needed in lists of nouns, adjectives, verbs or adverbs :

> Onion, potatoes, tomatoes and sugar are in short supply.
>
> The school was long, boring, tasteless, and badly directed.
>
> The children laughed, cheered and shouted.

It should be sung softly, gently and lightly.

A comma before *and* introducing the final item in a list is optional but normally unnecessary. There is no need for commas when a list of adjectives precedes a noun in a flowing way:

A big old ambassador car drew up alongside.

but commas help emphasis if adjectives gel with each other:

A tall, gaunt, untidy-looking young man.

The comma is also used in a list of phrases or clauses (main on subordinate) :

His favourite hobbies are listening to music, gardening, and playing in the weekends. (*phrases*)

We went to a club, spent a long time over the bar, and talked of old times. (*main clauses*)

He said that he had bought the house as a ruin, renovated it at considerable expenses, and then sold it. (*subordinate clauses*)

In such longer constructions, a comma before and introducing the final item is a helpful signpost, some people would argue that it is superfluous.

Marking off clauses

Use a pair of commas to separate information inserted into a sentence and which therefore interrupts the sense. Don't forget the second of the pair:

When the riots ceased after 5 long months, and after the gains and losses had been painfully reckoned, the bitter truth at last became known.

The dog, which until then had been sleeping, suddenly leapt to its feet.

Having managed to climb the ladder, though it had creaked ominously from time to time, he began to feel less apprehensive.

The comma is not always needed to mark off a clause or phrase: its assistance is seldom required in a simple construction.

When you come back it will be finished.

In all the excitement he had not noticed the time.

Even so, the lack of a comma in even a short sentence may cause momentary ambiguity or untidiness. In :

From the hill beyond the village looks smaller.

The reader get as far as *looks* before realizing that *village* is the subject of verb, not the object of *beyond*. A comma after *beyond* makes the structure clear.

Marking words in apposition

(,,) **Add a pair of commas to mark off words in apposition:**

The social worker, a man deeply interested in the sense of community, described the suburbs as being peopled by rootless beings, gypsies who have no tribe.

Marking parentheses

(,) Insert commas to mark off words which are not part of the central structure of a sentence but inserted by way of parenthesis. These include :

Additions such as *I think, in conclusion, of course, yes, no, isn't it, please, thank you*;

the names of persons being addressed;

exclamations which are part of a sentence;

linking adverbs (e.g. *however, moreover, therefore, perhaps, nevertheless*) and corresponding phrases (e.g. *on the other hand, on the whole, even so*) which relate a sentence to preceding one.

In all cases, commas should be used only when the sense of parenthesis is present.

Commas should not be used between subject and verb or to link two sentences, however short :

> Please come soon, I miss you.

> A meeting has been arranged, this will be held next week

In the first of these a dash should replace the comma, because the second statement explains the first.

In the second you could use a semicolon or a comma plus 'and', to indicate a relationship between the two statements. Alternatively, a full stop followed by a capital letter would be possible in both examples.

Most common mistake

Commas are often used in pairs to mark off parts of sentences. A common mistake is to forget the second comma:

Famine, as has often been noticed is prevalent in Rajasthan.

Dance classes, despite their popularity with younger members have had to be withdrawn.

Punctuation is needed after *noticed* and *members* to complete the parenthesis.

Hyphen

Hyphens are normally used after such prefixes as *vice* – (vice-captain), *ex-* (ex-serviceman), *self-* (self-conscious) and *non-* (non-starter), and are usually needed before *up* (close-up) and off (brush-*off*) in the formation of compound words. Thus

She gave him a brush-off.
        but
Brush off the dandruff.

Hyphens are always needed between a prefix and a proper noun:

pro-Indian, un-Indian, ex-President.

Compound adjectives are often made by combining adjectives and nouns:

middle-class values, *full-time* job, *short-term* prospects, *left-wing* views.

The hyphen is not used when such words are used as straightforward adjectives and nouns, not as compounds:

a town in the south, the left wing of the party.

In the same way, hyphens found in other compounds (*out-of-date computer*) should be dropped when the same words are used with their normal grammatical function (*The computer is out of date*).

Hyphens should always be used in words which, unhyphenated, would be ambiguous (*re-form*, *re-sign*, *re-cover*) or ugly (*full-length*, *semi-invalid*).

The writer has freedom to use more than one hyphen in the interests of clarity. A *semi-house trained dog* implies that there exists a trained dog capable of being described as semi-house. The correct punctuation is *semi-house-trained dog*.

Apostrophe

The apostrophe has two important functions:
  1. to indicate possession
  2. to mark the place where something has been left out of a shortened word.

Possession

Possession is denoted by adding an apostrophe followed by *s* to the end of a singular word :

The family's plans, the company's address, the politician's reputation

and an apostrophe without *s* to the end of a plural word ending in -s:

> ladies' shoes (i.e. shoes for *ladies*), the brothers' disagreement (i.e. the disagreement of the *brothers*)

This rule does not apply when a plural word does not end in -*s* (e.g. men, children, women). In such cases, the apostrophe followed by s is needed to denote possession:

men's trousers, *children's* toys, *women's* magazines

There is some disagreement should singular words end-ing in –*s*. Both *Sharmas' wife* and *Sharma's wife* are acceptable. The former is perfectly clear; the latter reflects normal pronunciation more accurately.

The modern preference for simplicity in punctuation favours the former:

Keats' poetry, Guy Fawkes' night.

An apostrophe is never used with possessive pronouns:

Hers, yours, theirs, his, ours, whose, its

The possessive *one's* needs an apostrophe; the plural *ones*, of course, does not:

One must do one's best.

Those are the ones I like.

The apostrophe should be used in:

a month's holiday, in a week's time, several years' imprisonment, a team's work, six hours' delay and in:

I must go to the barber. Their prices were lower then other companies'. (*short for the barber's shop* and *other companies' prices*)

The apostrophe is often omitted in the names of well-known firms:

Barclays Bank, Marks and *Spencers*

We do not to use an apostrophe after a plural noun that has an adjectival rather than a possessive sense :

Accounts Sections, Students Union, Social Services Department, Girls School

Shortened words

Words are sometimes shortened to effect the way they are commonly pronounced. The omitted letter are replaced by an apostrophe which, colloquially, marks the place in a word where something has been left out. Here are some examples:

> I am > *I'm*, it is > *it's*, you are > *you're*, we are > *we're*, they have > *they've*
>
> Do not> *don't*, shall not > *shan't*, would not > *wouldn't*, she will > *she'll*
>
> Cannot > *can't*, does not > *doesn't*, will not > *won't*; is not > *isn't*
>
> of the clock > o'clock; there is > there's; the summer of '98

Although short forms are general in speech and informal writing, one must be careful how to you use then when writing more formally. Some of them, *e.g. I'm*, *it's*, are very common,others are less acceptable.

In rare cases, the apostrophe is used to form plurals:

> do's and don'ts, the three R's, p's and q's, dot the i's and cross the t's

The apostrophe denoting the plural should not be used after numbers and abbreviations:

the 1990s, Congress MPs, temperature in the 80's.

Most common mistake

It is very common to put an apostrophe in words where there should not be one.

Capital letters

Capital letters are needed at the beginnings of sentences, and in direct speech. They are also used for proper nouns and titles.

Proper nouns

Nouns naming particular people (*The Queen of England*) and groups of people (*the Indians*), places (*the Hills of Shimla*), rivers, buildings (*City Town Hall*), institutions (*the Catholic Church*), establishments (*Apollo Hospital*), firms (*Tata Motors*), organizations (*the National Book Trust*). Countries, towns, streets, months of the year, days of the week, festivals (*Christmas, Diwali, Easter*), mountains, pets, house names, etc. Adjectives formed from proper nouns have capital letters (*German, Shakespearean*).

Titles

The titles of books, films, plays, television programmes, newspapers, magazines , songs, etc. The first word of a title always has a capital; unimportant words in the title (of, the, in, and) are generally spelt without one (*Gone with the Wind, Lord of the Flies*). The titles of people have capital letters (*The Lord Chancellor*).

It is normal practice to use capital letters for the particular, and small letters for the general:

The Queen of England	*but*	the kings and queens of England
The Speaker of the House	*but*	He was made a speaker
South India	*but*	We drove south
Delhi University	*but*	He had a university education
The Government	*but*	governments since 1947

Other Subtler Punctuations

Colon (:)

The colon is a sharp punctuation. It carries the general sense of 'that is to say', and has a number of uses.

Introducing a list

To introduce a list when the sense demands a pause: The house has a number of plus points: a swimming pool, a lawn, pent-house and a pool side bar.

Anticipating an explanation

Use a colon to point forward an example or an explanation.

Leading up to a climax

Use it before a word or words which have a sense of climax or need emphasis.

Making a dramatic break

Use a colon rather than a comma when you want to make a sharper, more dramatic break between the introduction and the quotation or title.

The colon and dash (:-) is an unnecessary punctuation. The colon on its own is sufficient.

Semicolon (;)

The semi colon is stronger than the comma and weaker than the full stop in the length of pause or degree of separation it imposes.

Joining two sentences

Use a semicolon when you wish to join two sentences, especially short ones, to make a longer statement. It is especially useful when there is an element of comparison:

> Reading is good; writing is better.

Use a semi-colon rather than a comma before such linking words as *besides, however, nevertheless, as a result, for example, as a consequence, in any case.*

Hyphen

The hyphen joins two or three words into single entity:

Sister-in-law, get-together

Also helps to prevent ambiguity:

> *extra-marital sex*

Also used in numbers and fractions

> *Four-and-a-half hour meeting*

Also used in compound adjectives

> *blue-eyed*

Dashes

A single dash marks a sharp break in the sentences

> *I warned him- but he would not listen*!

A pair of dashes is used when inserting a piece of information into a sentence, for stronger emphasis

> *Rohan- an utter crook- is sitting over there.*

Quotation marks

Quotation marks are also known as inverted commas or speech marks. They are used to mark:

1. Direct speech
2. Title of poems, plays, songs, etc.
3. Words referred to as words

MORE ON USAGE

Nouns

1. *Nouns Always Singular.* Note: certain nouns commonly used in English—advice, furniture, information, luggage, news, nonsense, progress, rubbish, weather—are always singular and follow the rule for uncountable nouns (e.g. bread, milk, ink, etc.) in *not* taking the indefinite article and in being used alone, or with "the", "some", "any".

Wrong (W).	What a nonsense to have a cricket match in such a bad weather!
	He hasn't a decent furniture in his house.
	The news are good today.

Right (R).	What nonsense to have a cricket match in such bad weather!
	He hasn't any decent furniture in his house.
	The news is good today.

Comment(C) If we wish to emphasize the singular aspect of these nouns we must say—a *piece* of advice, furniture, information, luggage, news, nonsense rubbish. (Note—a spell of weather.)

2. *Nouns Always Plural.* Note that other nouns—amends, braces, compasses, glasses (spectacles), goods, means, people, pliers, police, premises, scissors, statistics, thanks, tongs, trousers, and certain descriptive adjectives used as nouns (the blind, the guilty, etc.)—are always plural.

W.	If your braces is loose your trousers comes down.
	This premises looks too big.
	Is the old always wiser than the young?
R.	If your braces are loose your trousers come down.
	These premises look too big.
	Are the old always wiser than the young?

| C. | If we wish to make a singular from the last group we must say "the old man", "the young man", etc. Note — the singular of "police" is "policeman" (or "policewoman"!) and that we speak of a pair of compasses, glasses, pliers, scissors, spectacles, tongs or trousers. |

3. *Collective Nouns.* These can be singular or plural according to context, so don't forget to use your commonsense Don't make them singular when the context demands plural, or vice versa.

W.	The football team is having its bath.
	The committee are resolved upon this reform.
R.	The football team are having their bath.
	The committee is resolved upon this reform.
C.	When you think of the team or committee as *one body* of people, use the singular; when you think of the *different* people who make up the team or committee, use the plural.

4. *Compound Nouns.* Don't try and make false plurals here.

| W. | This man hates all women—mother-in-laws, woman-teachers, ladies-doctors, and houses-maids. |
| R. | This man hates all women—mothers-in-law, women-teachers, lady-doctors and house-maids. |

C.	The rule is : (i) Compound nouns made up of two nouns take the plural in the second noun only, except when the first noun is "man" or "woman", then both nouns take the plural form, e.g. tooth-brush, tooth-brushes, but man-servant, men-servants. (ii) Compound nouns with a preposition take the plural only in the first noun, e.g. man-of-war, men-of-war, son-in-law, sons-in-law.

5. *Possessive Case of Nouns.* (a) There are important exceptions to the general rule of using the possessive case only with nouns denoting animate or personified objects.

W.	Her house's number was at the front-door's side, which was a walk of five minutes from the house where I was spending a holiday of a month.
R.	The number of her house was at the side of the front-door, which was five minutes' walk from the house where I was spending a month's holiday.
C.	Exceptions — when the possessive case is used for inanimate objects in certain expression, mainly that of time, distance or money.

    a fortnight's holiday
    a stone's throw

and in these idiomatic expressions:

    at my wit's end
    out of harm's way

> to his heart's content
> in his mind's eye
> at his finger's ends
> for goodness' sake
> for conscience' sake
> the sun's rays

In poetry too, inanimate possessive is often used where prose would demand "of". Personification plays a large part here.

(b) *Names*. Don't forget that names ending in –*s* must omit the extra *s* if they are classical, and may omit the extra *s* if they are unusual.

> Argus' eyes (classical name).
>
> Keats' poems or Keats's poems (unusual name)

(c) *Group Genitives*. When several words are in apposition be careful to form their possessive with the *'s* on the last word *only if you are sure that they form a single sense unit and the result is free from ambiguity*.

W.	Adam's and Eve's children.
	Browning and Tennyson's poetry.
	Beaumont's and Fletcher's plays.
R.	Adam and Eve's children. (single sense unit)
	Browning's and Tennyson's poetry. (separate)
	Beaumont and Fletcher's plays. (single sense unit)
C.	Clumsiness and ambiguity are very common faults when possessives are used in groups or lists.

(d) Notice that certain adjectives used as nouns cannot take a possessive in *'s*, although they denote persons.

| W. | The rich's hobbies and the old's senility. |
| R. | The hobbies of the rich and the senility of the old. |

PRONOUNS

1. *Objective after Verb "To Be"*. Don't write, or say, "It's I!" Remember that personal pronouns can take the objective case in predicative or exclamatory use.

e.g. It's me!
      It wasn't him.
      Dear me, what a shame!

2. *Them*. Avoid using "*them*" as if it were a demonstrative adjective.

| W. | Give me them books. |
| R. | Give me those books. |

3. *They*. Don't use "*they*" as an antecedent to "who" or "that".

| W. | They who go by train must leave now. |
| R. | Those who go by train must leave now. |

4. *That*. Don't use "*that*" as a relative pronoun (a) after a preposition, (b) in a Non- defining Relative.

| W. | Here is the book of that I told you. |

My father, that works in a bank, is now on holiday.

R.	Here is the book that I told you of. Or Here is the book of which I told you.

My father, who works in a bank, in now on holiday.

5. *What*. Don't use "*what*" as a relative pronoun with an antecedent.

W.	The novel what I read was good.
R.	The novel that I read was good.
	Or (without antecedent), What I read was good.

6. *Who*. Don't use "*who*" as a relative pronoun if the antecedent is used with "all", "any", "only", "it is", or a superlative. Custom here prefers "that".

W.	It was only Smith who stayed away.
	He was the best teacher who ever lived.
R.	It was only Smith that stayed away.
	He was the best teacher that ever lived.

7. *Whom*. (a) Remember to use "whom" only when it is the object of its clause or sentence.

W.	That is a girl whom we all agree is very beautiful.
R.	That is the girl who we all agree is very beautiful.

(b) Avoid "than whom"

W.	"Pope than whom few men had more vanity"
R.	"Few men had more vanity than Pope".

8. *Reflexive and Emphatic Pronoun*. Don't make a reflexive or emphatic pronoun stand alone as the subject of a verb. Give it its accompanying noun or pronoun.

W.	Herself saw the thief.
	Sandeepa and myself will come.
R.	She herself saw the theif.
	Sandeepa and I myself will come.

9. *Singular Pronouns*. Note— "none", "neither", "any", "each" and "everyone" are singular. Don't ever try making them plural.

W.	None of these girls are here.
	Everyone must do their duty.
	Neither of his parents are British.
R.	None of these girl is here.
	Everyone must do his duty (or her duty).
	Neither of his parents is British.

10. *Each Other, One Another*. Note —"each other" is used when there are two objects, "one another" when there are more than two.

W.	He was so afraid that his knees knocked one another.

He and his four brothers love each other very much.

R.	He was so afraid that his knees knocked each other.

He and his four brothers love one another very much.

11. *Unattached and Wrongly Attached Pronouns.*

W.	"If the baby does not digest fresh milk, it should be boiled."
R.	"If the baby does not digest fresh milk, the milk should be boiled."

ADJECTIVES

1. *Many, Much.*

W.	He ate many biscuits and drank much coffee.
R.	He ate a large number of biscuits and drank a great deal of coffee.
C.	"Many" is used
	(1) in interrogative and negative sentences,
	(2) as the subject or part of the subject, and
	(3) in the expressions—a good many, a great many, so many, too many, how many, as many, many a.
	In all other cases replace it by –" a lot of", " a great number of", "a large number of", "plenty of".

"Much" follows the same rules, and is replaced by—"a lot of", "a great deal of", and "plenty of".

2. *Few, Little.* Note—these imply a negative meaning ("not many", "not much") unless preceded by the indefinite article.

| W. | He has saved hard and now has little money. |

He is not lonely for he has few friends.

| R. | He has saved hard and now has a little money. |

He is not lonely, for he has a few friends.

3. *Due to, Owing to.* To understand the difference between the use of "due to" and "owing to", it may be helpful to *keep in mind* the following "rule":

Due to (meaning "caused by") is associated with parts of the verb *to be* as an adjectival complement; e.g.

His illness *was* due to his overeating.

Was the trouble due to any misunderstanding on our part?

Owing to (meaning "because of") is a prepositional phrase governing nouns and nominals ; it is likely to come at the beginning of a sentence; e.g.

Owing to his poor English, he failed in all papers.

Owing to the bad weather, no planes left in the morning.

No planes left in the morning (because of) owing to the bad weather.

4. *Like.* Avoid using this adjective as a conjunction.

W.	Her hair is brown, like her mother's is.
R.	Her hair is brown, like her mother's.
	Or, her hair is brown, as her mother's is.

5. *Comparison*. Be careful here as errors are frequently made in the comparison of adjectives.

(a) *Impossible Comparison*.   Don't give comparatives or superlatives to adjectives that do not admit of degree of comparison, e.g. unique, eternal, triangular, weekly, monthly.

(b) *Double Comparison*. Avoid using "more" and then a comparative.

W.	They are more kinder to animals than to children.
	It is more profitable to sell in Delhi rather than to sell here.
R.	They are kinder to animals than to children.
	It is more profitable to sell in Delhi than to sell here.

(c) *Wrongly Formed Comparison*.   Don't add *–er*, *-est* to adjectives of more than two syllabus.

Remember that "shy, shyer, shyest" is the exception to the rule of *y* after a consonant changing to *i* in the comparative and superlative of adjectives of one or two syllables. ("Dry" and "sly" sometimes follow the rule and sometimes copy "shy".) Also several short words "real", "right", "wrong", "like" and all adjectives of nationality form their comparatives with "more" and their superlatives with "most".

W.	She is intelligenter, but shier than her sister.
	This portrait looks realler than the other.
R.	She is more intelligent, but shyer than her sister.
	This portrait looks more real than the other.

Notice too that certain adjectives, with the superlative in *–most*, have no comparative-degree form:

Eastern	easternmost
End	endmost
Head	headmost
Left	leftmost
Middle	middlemost
Northern	northernmost
Rear	rearmost
Right	rightmost
Southern	southernmost
Top	topmost

(d) *Latin Comparatives.* Remember that certain adjectives of Latin origin—anterior, inferior, posterior, prior, senior, superior (they can be recognized by their *–or* ending instead of *–er*) –are followed by "to" and not "than".

W.	Her work is superior than her brother's although he is senior than her at college.
R.	Her work is superior to her brother's although he is senior to her at college.

| C. | "preferable" also takes "to". e.g. This novel is preferable to that. |

(e). *Twofold Comparisons.* Distinguish between: *latter*, *last* and *later*, *latest* (from late). "Later" and "Last" refer to *order*; "Later" and "latest" to time. "Latter" is never used with "than".

Older, *oldest* and *elder*, *eldest*. "Older" and "oldest" refer to the age of persons or things; "elder" and "eldest" refer to persons only and are used in reference to order to birth in a family. e.g. He was the eldest son, but as his brothers, outlived him, he was not always the oldest.

Farther, *farthest* and *further*, *furthest* (from far). "Farther" and "farthest" refer to distance only; " further" and "furthest" refer to distance and addition. e.g. I will give you further information (not *farther*).

(f) *Superlative for Comparative.* Don't use the superlative while referring to only two persons or things.

| W. | This novel is the best of the two. |
| R. | This novel is the better of the two. |

(g) *More.* Don't forget that the rule is to use "more" when two qualities of the same person or thing are compared.

W.	This little girl is better than clever.
R.	This little girl is more good than clever.
C.	In speaking of two dimensions, however, the normal comparative may be used. e.g. This window is wider than it is high.

(h) *Other*. Use "other" with comparatives when necessary (but never with superlatives).

W.	Her autobiography is more interesting than any book I have read.
	I believe he is more evil than any living man.
R.	Her autobiography is more interesting than any other book I have read.
	I believe he is more evil than any other living man.
C.	The person or thing compared must obviously be excluded from the classes of persons or things with which it is being compared, and so the use of "other" or "else" or some such word is necessary here.

(6). *Order of Adjectives*. Remember there are a few exceptions to the rule of the adjective preceding its noun:

e.g. court martial   notary public

      heir apparent   Poet Laureate

Notice too that the following adjectives are generally used predicatively; if used attributively *they always follow the noun*:

afraid	ashamed	awake
akin	askew	aware
alike	asleep	awry
alive	athirst	extinct
alone	averse	ill

W.	An afraid soldier is a sorry spectacle.
	An alone lady might be in danger here.
R.	A soldier afraid (who is afraid) is a sorry spectacle.
	A lady alone (who is alone) might be in danger here.

VERBS

1. *Present Perfect*. Be careful of the tenses.

(a) Don't use it for a finished action when a definite time is stated.

W.	I have visited Australia last August.
	He has ridden a scooter three years ago.
R.	I visited Australia last August.
	He rode a scooter three years ago.
C.	An exception occurs when the Present Perfect is used for a finished action when the period of time stated is *not yet completed*.
	e.g. I have read four books this week. (Week not yet finished.)
	He has seen her this evening. (Evening not yet finished.)

(b) Always use the Present Perfect and not the Present Simple with *Since* and *For*, when measuring time up to the present.

W.	I am here since 1998.
	He doesn't write to you for a week.
R.	I have been here since 1998.
	He hasn't written to you for a week.
C.	"Since" here denotes—from some definite point or period in past time until now "For" here denotes—length of time until now.

Notice that if "since", with this meaning, governs a clause, the verb in that clause must be in the Past tense.

W.	I haven't eaten biscuits since I have been a child.
R.	I haven't eaten biscuits since I was a child.

(c) *Already, Just, Not yet, Now*. Notice the use of the Present Perfect with these adverbials of present time, to denote a finished action with emphasis on the present state of completion.

W.	She didn't yet see the film star.
	He finished his lunch now and is satisfied.
R.	She hasn't yet seen the film star.
	He has finished his lunch now and is satisfied.

(2.) *Future*. (a) Don't use a Future tense when a present meaning is really intended.

W.	We shall look forward to seeing you.
	I shall accept your invitation with pleasure. (in a letter of acceptance.)

| R. | We look forward (or are looking forward) to seeing you. |
| | I accept your invitation with pleasure. |

(b) Don't use a Future tense after temporal conjunctions—until, when, before, after, as soon as.

W.	He will come when he will be ready.
	They will write as soon as they will arrive home.
R.	He will come when he is ready.
	They will write as soon as they arrive home.

(c) Don't confuse "*shall*" and "*will*". Remember that "shall" (1st person) and "will" (2nd and 3rd persons) indicate a plain future, and the reverse—"will" (1st person) and "shall" (2nd and 3rd persons) indicate a future coloured by ideas of *Purpose*, *Resolution*, *Determination* and (in the negative) *Restraint*.

(d) Don't use "will" for questions in the first person. We rarely ask someone else about our own will.

| W. | Will I give you the newspaper? |
| R. | Shall I give you the newspaper? |

(e) Don't believe that the Future tense has any real future meaning in sentences like these:

(1) You will all have heard of Tagore.

(2) You will have seen the page is missing.

(3) This will be the way.

C. This is called the future of Assumption, and is quite commonly used, especially in speeches, lectures and debates. The meaning is: I *assume* or I *expect* or I *imagine* or I take it that.

(1) You have heard of Tagore.

(2) You have seen that the page is missing.

(3) This is the way.

3. *Unreal Past.* Don't use the future or the Present tense after such expressions as—suppose (that), it's time (that), if only, as if, I'd rather (that), I wish that:

W.	It's high time that you go home.
	I'd rather you will take my brother to the dinner tonight.
	If only he can swim!
R.	It's time that you went home.
	I'd rather you took my brother to dinner tonight.
	If only he could swim!
C.	These expressions govern a past tense known as the Unreal or Imaginative Past. The Past Simple is used for something wished for or supposed now, and the Past Perfect when the wish or supposition is all in the apt.

e.g. If only I had a car! (Now)

If only I had had a car! (Yesterday)

3. *Conditionals.* Don't confuse the sequence of tenses in conditional sentences.

W.	If he has time he would telephone.
	They don't come if they hear this.
	He would have gone if she wanted.
R.	If he has time he will telephone.
	They won't come if they hear this.
	He would have gone if she had wanted.
C.	Notice the three main types of conditional sentences:

(1) He will answer if you write to him.

(*Open Condition.* Main Clause—Future, "if" clause—Present.)

(2) He would answer if you wrote to him.

(*Imaginary Condition.* Main Clause—Conditional, "if" clause—Past.)

(3) He would have answered if you had written to him. (*Impossible condition.* Main Clause—conditional perfect, "if" clause—Past Perfect.)

Exceptions. There are, however, some important exceptions to the Open Condition rule.

(a) *Cause and Effect.* Same tenses in both clauses.

People die if they drink this spurious liquor.

If you mix flour and water you make a paste.

(b) *Fact and Not True Condition.* Same tense in both clauses.

If you are a coward, I am not!

(I am certain that you are a coward!)

(c) *Polite Forms.* When asking for someone's consent or co-operation, use the future tense in both clauses.

If you'll wait here, I'll get my bat.

(d) *Doubt and Improbability.* A doubtful opinion is sometimes expressed by using "should" or "were to" in the "if" clause.

If he should refuse (or—should he refuse) I shall be angry.

(But I doubt if he will refuse.) If she were to die now what must I do? (But her immediate death is unlikely.)

(5) *Can.* Don't use "could" for the Past tense of "can" when the meaning is "to manage to", to attain to through an effort".

W.	I could pass my examination two years ago.
	When my father died I could continue business.
R.	I was able to pass my examination two years ago.
	When my father died I was able to continue his business.
C.	"Could" and "was able to" are usually interchangeable, except in when "was able to" must be used, and in the meaning of *permission,* when "could" must be used. e.g. He said that I *could* go.

(6) *Have.* Don't conjugate "have" with "do" when it means "to possess on some specified occasion".

| W. | He doesn't have a cold today. |

Does he have any hope of passing his examination next week?

R.   He hasn't a cold today.

Has he any hope of passing his examination next week?

C.   "Have" is conjugated without "do" in the above meaning, and when used as an auxiliary; "have" is conjugated with "do" when it means: "to experience", "to eat", "to drink", "to receive" or "to take".

W.   Generally she hasn't headaches.

Have you difficulty with your car?

Have you breakfast at eight?

We have not coffee for breakfast.

They have not parcels from home.

He has not a bath every day.

R.   Generally she doesn't have headaches.

Do you have breakfast at nine?

We do not have coffee for breakfast.

They do not have parcels from home.

He does not have a bath every day.

(7) *Verb Patterns*. Don't confuse your verb patterns. A common mistake is to use an infinitive construction with verbs that demand a gerundial construction.

W.   I enjoy to learn English.

He avoids to speak to me.

	He has finished to study.
R.	I enjoy learning English.
	He avoids speaking to me
	He has finished studying .
C.	Here is a list of the most important verbs that take a gerundial construction. Those marked with an asterisk can also take an infinitive.

avoid	imagine	risk
begin*	intend*	stop
continue*	keep (continue)	can't bear
delay	like*	can't help
detest	love*	can't stand
dread	miss	don't mind
enjoy	postpone	it needs*

Another common error is the use of an accusative and infinitive construction instead of a "that" construction, and vice versa.

W.	My mother wants that I come home.
	Rita suggested me to do it.
	Now she orders that I come.
	I don't intend that I obey.
R.	My mother wants me to come hom.
	Rita suggested to me that I should do it.
	Now she orders me to come.
	I don't intend to obey.

| C. | | Some of the more important verbs that normally take an accusative and infinitive construction and not a "that" construction are: |

allow	intend	permit
ask	invite	want
encourage	Force	watch*

Those normally taking a "that" construction and not an accusative and infinitive are:

admit	explain	maintain
agree	ensure	propose
decide	hold	say
demand	inform	suggest

Those taking either an accusative and infinitive or a "that" construction are:

Advise	feel[1]	see[1]
Assume	find	teach
Believe	hear[1]	tell
Calculate	know	show
Choose	persuade	think
Consider	prove	trust
Declare	reckon	understand
Discover	remind	warn
Expect	reveal	wish

---

[1]*These verbs take the infinitive without "to"*

8. *Misrelated Participles*: Avoid the misrelated participle, otherwise known as the confused, dangling, disconnected, suspended, unattached, unrelated or wandering participle.

W.	Being home a wet day, he stayed at home.
	Removed to the country, we believe that the animals will be happier.
	Born of a humble family, Fate yet bestowed him many gifts.
R.	As it was a wet day, he stayed at home.
	We believe that the animals will be happier if removed to the country.
C.	Do not confuse these with absolute construction, which are grammatically correct.
	e.g. All things considered, the party was a success.

9. *Error of Proximity*. Don't refer the verb to a wrong subject—usually an intervening plural.

W.	Nothing but trees and fields lie before our gaze.
	Not a line of these lectures have been prepared.
R.	Nothing but trees and fields lies before our gaze.
	Not a line of these lectures has been prepared.

ADVERBS

1. *Quite*. Don't use this adverb as if it were an adjective.

W.	He has made quite a fortune.
	You gave me quite a shock!
R.	He has made a substantial fortune.
	You gave me a big shock!
C.	"Quite" means "perfectly" or "entirely".
	"Quite so"as a response means "I entirely agree", or "I grant you the truth of that".

2. *Adverbial Order*. Although this is fairly elastic in English, be careful not to break the few rules that there are.

W.	He comes late often to school.
	She sang last night beautifully at the concert.
R.	He often comes to school late.
	She sang beautifully at the concert last night.
C.	The usual position of adverbs and adverbial phrases and clauses is at the end of a sentence and in the order *manner*, *place* and *time*.

Exceptions. (a) After verbs of motion adverbial expression of *place* usually come next to the verb.

> e.g.   He went home by bus.

(b) Certain adverbs such as "already", "almost", "just", "nearly". "quite", "hardly", "scarcely", and all *frequency adverbs* (i.e. those answering the question "how often?"— "always", "frequently", "generally" "never", "often", "sometimes", "usually") come *before* the principal verb, except the verb "*to be*". They come after the verb "to be", and after the auxiliaries.

> e.g. Tina is always early.
>
> Tina has always been early.
>
> Tina always comes early.
>
> Tina will always come early.

(c) Adverbial expression of *time* are often placed at the beginning of a sentence. Notice that the more particular expression of time are usually placed before the more general.

> e.g. At five o'clock in the morning she began to play that music system.
>
> Yesterday we went to the studio.

(d) Adverbs generally come *before* adjectives, past participles and other adverbs.

> e.g. He is extremely clever and will educated, but very badly dressed.

Notice however that "enough" does *not* follow this rule and comes after the adjective, past participle or other adverb.

> e.g. She is not good enough at badminton; she has not practiced enough and does not run quickly enough.

3. *Only.* False positioning here is also responsible for many common errors.

W.   One student only came in late yesterday.

	He only married her for her money.
R.	Only one student came in late yesterday.
	He married her only for her money.
C.	This word must go immediately before the word or phrase that it is intended to qualify, or it will produce the wrong effect.

Notice the naughty (ONLY)

Only he said he loved her

He only said he loved her

He said only he loved her

He said he only loved her

He said he loved only her

He said he loved her only

4. *Hardly, Scarcely.* Don't use a negative with these adverbs they already possess a negative meaning.

W.	I don't hardly know this woman.
	He can't scarcely see in this light.
R.	I hardly know this woman.
	He can scarcely see in this light.

5. *Badly.* Notice that this adverb, when used with "need" and "want", usually precedes the verb and has the meaning of "urgently".

W.	Your hair needs cutting badly.
	Your hair badly needs cutting.

PREPOSITIONS

1. *Sequence of Prepositions.* Certain parts of speech, particularly verbs, adjectives and nouns, require special prepositions, and the mastery of these is one of the most difficult tasks for the student of English. Here is a list of the some important prepositional constructions.

(a) Prepositions with Verbs

(Against)
guard
lean
offend
rebel
warn

(At)
Aim
gaze
glance
hint
jeer
jump
laugh
look
peck
smile
stare
wonder

(From)
hinder
prevent

protect
recover
refrain
save
separate
subtract
absolve
abstain
alight
benefit
borrow
derive
desist
differ
digress
emerge
escape
exclude

(For)
apologize
beg
care
charge

compensate
cry
feel
forgive
hope
long
mourn
pine
pray
punish
send
strive
sue
wait
weep
wish

(Of)

acquit
accuse
admit
approve
become
beware
boast
complain
convince
despair
die
dispose
dream
head
suspect

smell
repent
think
clear

(In)

abound
believe
delight
excel
fail
increase
indulge
involve
persevere
persist
revel
succeed

(On)

base
bestow
comment
congratulate
decide
depend
feast
frown
impose
insist
intrude
operate
reflect

rely
resolve
spend

(With)
coincide
comply
compromise
copy
disagree
dispense
fill
grapple
interfere
meddle
part
quarrel
supply
sympathize
threaten
unite

(To)
abandon
accede
adapt
add
adhere
allude
amount
aspire
attach
attend

belong
commit
confine
conform
consent
consign
contribute
drink
introduce
liken
listen
object
subject
surrender
yield

Notice these pairs:

agree with (a person)
agree to (a thing)
part from (a person)
part with (a thing)
reconcile to (a person)
reconcile with (a thing)
interfere with (a person)
interfere in (a thing)
compare to (asserting similarity)
compare with (seeking similarity)
deal with (a person)
deal in (a thing)

(b) Prepositions with Adjectives (including Participles)

(At)
amazed
amused
clever
quick
slow
stupid

(For)
celebrated
destined
eager
eligible
fit
hungry
prepared
qualified
ready
responsible
sorry
suitable
useful
(From)
absent
different
exempt
far
free
inseparable
remote
safe

separate

(in)
absorbed
accurate
backward
deficient
dressed
servile
interested
involved
poor
rich

(Of)
afraid
ashamed
aware
capable
conscious
deprived
devoid
envious
expressive
fond
full
guilty
independent
innocent
jealous
observant

proud
shy
sick
suspicious
tired
worthy

(On)
bent
determined
keen
intent
dependent

(To)
accustomed
agreeable
applicable
blind
condemned
conductive
contrary
engaged
equivalent
faithful
fatal
foreign
hostile
inferior
incidental
indifferent
indulgent
favourable

known
loyal
married
new
opposite
painful
partial
polite
profitable
prone
related
similar
superior
true

(with)
afflicted
busy
content
delighted
disgusted
endowed
faint
familiar
inconsistent
inspired
patient
pleased
popular
satisfied
Notice:
angry
annoyed

With (a person)
furious
At (a thing)
irritated
vexed
good
At (an occupation)
bad
To (a person)

For (a person)
disappointed of (what we cannot get)
disappointed in (what we have got)
glad at (a piece of news)
gald of (a possession)

(c) Preposition with Nouns

(For)
affection
apology
appetite
blame
contempt
desire
fondness
gratitude
leisure
liking
passion
pretext
reputation
In (without article) or Of (with article)
Confidence
Delight
Difficulty

Happiness
Joy
Pleasure
Pride
Satisfaction
skill
(From)
deliverance
descent
escape
exemption
release

(Of)
abhorrence
dislike
distrust
experience
evasion

neglect
proof
result
sense
victim
view
want
witness

(On)
decision
dependence
expenditure
influence
meditation
reflection

(With)
accordance
acquaintance

antipathy
approach
attitude
contrast
cruelty
danger
disgrace
encouragement
exception
invitation
limit
menace
obedience
objection
obstruction
opposition
resemblance
slave
traitor

Note: (a) a martyr for (a cause), to (a disease).

(b) *In* the circumstances, not *under* the circumstances. (Circum means "round", and what is round is not over. Even good grammararians are sometimes guilty of this mistake.

(c) *In* a ship rather than *on* a ship. "In" is the preposition generally used by sailors and found in the writings of our nautical authors and master mariners. But notice "on board".

2.   *Some Pairs*. Don't confuse

(a) *Among and Between*

W.	It was a secret among my parents, not to be circulated between my brothers and sisters.
R.	It was a secret between my parents, not to be circulated among my brothers and sisters.
C.	"Between" is used for two, "among" for more than two objects, except in geographical use, when "between" can be used for more than two objects.

e.g. Switzerland lies between France, Germany and Italy.

(b) *Beside and Besides*

W.	Beside his Aunt he has six other female relations. "Oh, I do like to be besides the sea-side !"
R.	Besides his Aunt he has six other female relations. "Oh, I do like to be beside the sea-side!"
C.	"Beside" means "next to", " near", "at the side of". "Besides" means "as well as", "in addition to".

(c) *Into and In to*. Be careful to write the two words separately when the sense is separate.

W.	Lord Brown took her into dinner.
R.	Lord Brown took her in to dinner.

(d) *Under* and *Underneath*

W.	A Major is underneath a General.
R.	A Major is under a General.
C.	"Underneath" is used in a physical sense only.

SOME PHRASES WITH PREPOSITIONS

A

Abandon to	The prince abandoned his ministers to the fury of the mob.
Abide by	If you do not abide by the regulations, you will get in trouble.
Abhorrence of	Most people have an abhorrence of snakes.
Abstain from	The minister abstained from voting.
Accede to	The supervisor graciously acceded to my request.
Access to	Only graduate students have access to the library shelves.
Acclimate to	Have you become acclimated to this city?
Accountable to for	A worker is always accountable to his superior for his acts.

Acquaint with	Travel will acquaint you with new customs.
Acquit of	The jury acquitted him of any guilt in the matter.
Adapt for	Shakespeare's plays have been adapted for children.
Adapt to	You should adapt yourself to new ways of looking at matters.
Adept in	A politician becomes adept in agreeing with everybody.
Adhere to	You should always adhere to the truth.
Adverse to	I am adverse to bringing up the matter again.
Affix to	Affix the stamp to upper right corner of the envelope.
Agree to	The boys agreed to do what I asked.
Agree with	They agree with their partners on some metters.
Alien to	Such an attitude is alien to my philosophy.
Allergic to	Are you allergic to certain animals?
Allude to	Kapoor alluded to his difficulties with his mother-in-law.
Anxiety about	Wadhwa is anxious about her son.

Appetite for	Exercise will increase your appetite for food.
Ascribe to	We ascribed his rudeness to his fatigue.
Aspire to	Prasad did not aspire to a better position in life.
Assent to	The chairman assented to the proposal.
Asset to	Khanna is an asset to his company.
Assiduous in	Sumit is assiduous in his studies.
Attitude toward	Your attitude toward your duty is commendable.
Attribute to	Punctuality is an attribute of a good student.
Averse to	Rohit is not averse to working hard.
Aversion to	Rohit has no aversion to working hard.

B

Band against	The neighbours banded against the new arrival.
Bank on	If Narayanan gave you his promise, you can bank on getting the job.
Bear with "be patient with"	You should bear with the child while he is sick.

Behaviour toward	Vineet's behaviour toward his father was not respectful
Belong to	Those books belong to my brother.
Benefit from	Did you benefit from the lecture today?
Bequeath to	Vikram bequeathed his property to his eldest son.
Better off "in a better condition"	You will be better off in your new job.
Blush at	The young girl blushed at the joke.
Boast of (or about)	A wise man does not boast of his knowledge.
Brag about (or of)	A gentleman does not brag about his accomplishments.
Break in	1. "tame" That horse was wild, but the cowboy broke him in.
	2. "train" Her job is breaking new workers in.
	3. "make comfortable through use (said of shoes)" She asked her younger sister to break her new shoes in.
	4. "put into operation gradually" People used to have to break their cars in by driving slowly for the first thousand miles.

	5. "enter illegally" The robbers broke in the house.
Brood over	Don't worry so much. Don't brood over your troubles.
Burden with	I have enough troubles. Please don't burden me with yours.
Burst out (laughing or crying) "suddenly begin (to laugh or cry)"	The girl burst out crying when she saw me.
By and by "soon; later"	Father will be home from the office by and by.
By and large "in general; usually"	Goyal has some faults, but, by and large, he's a decent fellow.
By oneself "alone; without help"	He made the book case all by himself.

C

Call down "reprimand"	Aren't you ashamed that your teacher had to call you down for talking too much?
Call for	1. "come to get" Please be ready when I call for you tonight so we can leave right away.
	2. "require; demand" Chess calls for concentration and a good memory.
Call in "summon"	The chief called all the workers in for a conference.

Call off "cancel"	Rita called her party off because her mother got sick.
Call on	The teacher called on Rohan, but he could not answer correctly.
Called on (or upon) "oblighted"	I felt called on to express my opinion on the matter.
Call up	1. "telephone" Ramesh wants you to call him up. He left his number.
	2. "makes one remember" That song always calls up my first date.
Capacity of	This room has a capacity of forty-two seats.
Capacity for	Anu has no capacity for hard work.
Careful about (or of)	You should be more careful about your pronunciation.
Catch on	1. (to) "understand" We had to explain the joke to Karan because he could not catch on to it. Then, he said brightly, "Now I catch on!"
	2. "become popular" His new song caught on very fast.
Catch up (on) "become current; do what should have been done"	I was sick for a few days. Now I have got to catch up on my studying.

Cater to	That shop caters to wealthy people.
Caution about	My teacher has cautioned me about my spelling.
Caution against	My teacher has cautioned me against misspelling words.
Chagrin at	Arun was chagrined at losing the election.
Chance to	I want a chance to make some money.
Change for	Gupta has changed his old car for a new one.
Characteristic of	Punctuality is a characteristic of a conscientious student.
Characteristic by	His conversation is characterized by good humor.
Charge against	Every error will be charged against you.
Cheer up	"make or become happy" When I get despondent, my roommate cheers me up.
Choose between	You must choose between the two men. You can't marry both.
Coincide with	Tushar's statement coincided with mine.
Collide with	The bus collided with the streetcar.
Combine with	If you combine your savings with mine, we can buy a car.

Come around	1. "regain consciousness" She fainted, but she's coming around.
	2. "become agreeable" My wife is angry with me, but she'll come around me.
Come off "be successful; have the expected result"	The experiment did not come off.
Communicate with	about (or on) - I have communicated with my lawyer about the matter.
Commute between	Abhinav commutes between Noida and New Delhi Providence and New Haven every day.
Commute from to	Shetty commutes from his home to office every day.
Compensation, example… for	Did you receive any compensation for your work?
Compete with (or against) for	His store competes with ours for customers.
Compliment on	A number of people paid the author compliments on his novel.
Comply with	You should comply with the regulations.
Concede to	The candidate conceded victory to his opponent.
Conceited about	She shouldn't act proud: she hasn't anything to be conceited about.

Conclude by	He concluded by saying that the best thing was what we liked.
Conclusion, at the (of)	We took a vote at the conclusion of the debate.
Concur with—in	The chief justice concurred with his associates in the decision.
Condemn to	The criminal was condemned to death. He was condemned to die for his crime.
Confine to	Mathur is confined to his room by sickness.
Conform to	A citizen is expected to conform to the laws of his country.
Congratulate on	I want to congratulate you on your promotion.
Conscious of	The explorer was conscious of the natives' unfriendliness.
Consent, by common "unanimously"	Sharma was made chairman by common consent.
Consequence of	His defeat came as a consequence of his over-confidence.
Consign to	The merchandise has already been consigned to the department store.
Consistent in	A logical minded man tries to be consistent in his thoughts.
Consistent with	Your theory is not consistent with the facts.

Consort with	You can get a bad reputation from consorting with the wrong people.
Consult about	You should consult your doctor about your cough.
Contemptuous of	You should not be contemptuous of underprivileged people.
Contingent on (or upon)	The agreement was contingent on the stockholders' approval.
Contrary, on the	You think you are right, but, on the contrary, you're wrong.
Contrary to	Contrary to the weatherman's prediction, the day was fair.
Contrast between	The contrast between those two brothers is remarkable.
Convince by	I was convinced by his story.
Convince of	I want to convince you of his innocence; I am convinced of it.
Correspond to	This English expression correspond to that French one.
Courteous to	You should try to be courteous to everybody.
Covetous of	Dev was covetous of his neighbour's land.
Craving for	Do you have a craving for sweets?
Crazy about "fond of"	Teenage girls are crazy about that singer.
Credit of with	I have a credit of a hundred rupees with the bank.

Credit, on	You don't have to pay for that suit now. You can get it on credit.
Credit to	My deposit was credited to my account.
Cut down (on) "reduces"	I must cut down on my expenses somehow.
Cut in (on) "interrupt"	Don't cut in on your mother when she's talking.
Cut off	"stop" The girl tried to explain the mistake, but her father cut her off by saying that he was not interested.

D

Dabble in	Children like to dabble in water.
Dance to	The couple danced to the music for a while and then sat and listened.
Dash off	1. "leave hastily" Arjun dashed off without saying a word.
	2. "write hastily" I'll just dash a note off to my family.
Dawn on (or upon)	The idea dawned on him that the might be mistaken.
Day in, day out "continually"	Life is getting monotonous. I do the same things day in, day out.
Daybreak, at	The farmer began his work at daybreak.
Daze, in a "stupefied; confused"	Kapoor was in a daze after we told her the bad news.

Debate with on (or about)	I had a debate with the student on a grammatical item.
Debt, in	to for I am in debt to you for all your kindness.
Decent to	about The critics were decent to the author about his play.
Decide on (or upon)	Have you decided on the place you will go on your vacation?
Decrease from to	Their sales decreased from a thousand dollars to nine hundred.
Decrease in	There has been a decrease in sales recently.
Deduce from	The detective deduced from the clues that the suspect was innocent.
Defect in	That machine has a defect in its wiring.
Defer to	Young people are expected to defer to the wishes of their elders.
Deficient in	The native's diet was deficient in protein.
Defraud of	The financier defrauded the buyers of their savings.
Delegate to	An able administrator learns to delegate authority to his subordinates.
Delight in	A philatelist finds delight in stamps.
Delighted to	Verma was delighted to find his lost wallet.

Depend on (or upon) for	You can depend on me for assistance.
Dependent on (or upon) for	Bill is dependent on his parents for support.
Deprive of	The prisoners were deprived of food and water.
Derivative of	Coke is a derivative of coal.
Derive from	Coke is derived from coal.
Descendant of	French is a descendant of Latin.
Description of	The boy wrote a description of his home.
Desist from	We desisted from our work for a few.
Destined for	The ship was destined for London.
Destitute of	The shipwrecked sailors grew destitute of hope.
Deter from	I could not deter him from going.
Deterimental to	Laziness is detrimental to success.
Deviate from	A witness must not deviate from the truth.
Devoid of	I found the story completely devoid of interest.
Digress from	The speaker digressed from his topic for a few minutes.
Dint, by... of	The boys got through college by dint of sheer determination.
Disconcert by	I was disconcerted by her statement.

Discourse withon (or about)	We discoursed about the subject for a long time.
Discrepancy in	The prosecutor found a discrepancy in the witness's testimony.
Discrimination against	Vijay was accused of discrimination against Europeans.
Disparity in	The twins show a disparity in their abilities.
Dispense with "forgo; do without"	Since we don't have much time, we'll dispense with the reading today.
Dispose of	I must dispose of the garbage.
Dispute with on (or about)	The boy disputed with me about the date of the battle.
Dissent from	There were two dissents from the opinion.
Distaste for	The critic expressed his distaste for the book.
Distinct from	The language spoken today is quite distinct from the one spoken in the Middle Ages.
Distinguish between	It is difficult to distinguish between those twins.
Distinguish in	Herman distinguished himself in the contest.
Distrust of	Sarah developed a distrust of all strangers.
Diverge from	The path diverges from the river bank very soon.

Divest of	The aristocrats were divested of their property.
Doze off "begin to doze"	The child dozed off while I was reading to him.
Draw up "compose; write"	The director wants some new plans. Can you draw them up by tommorrow
Dream of (or about)	I had always dreamed about a trip to this country.
Drive at "try or intend to express"	That was the idea that Puneet was driving at.
Drive for	Let Mihir drive the car for you.
Drive to from	We drove to Jaipur from Delhi in a few hours.
Drop in (on) "visit without prior notice"	I am very busy; I hope nobody drops in on me tonight.
Drop out (of) "leave; quit attending"	He should not have dropped out.
Due to	The girl's absence is due to illness.
Dusk, at	The stars begin to appear at dusk.
Dwell on (or upon)	The teacher dwelled on the point to impress his students with its importance.

E

Eager to	I am eager to start my classes.

Earnest, in	Do you think Varun said that in earnest, or was he joking?
Ease, at "relaxed; comfortable"	I never feel at ease when Soni is around.
Ease, with	I can remember my grandfather with the greatest of ease.
East of	New York is east of Chicago.
Eat in "eat at home"	Are we eating in tonight?
Eat out "eat away from home"	Let's celebrate and eat out tonight.
Efficient in	My maid is efficient in everything she does.
Eligible for	Because of his good grades, Ashish is eligible for a prize.
Embodiment of	Manish is the embodiment of good manners.
Embody in	The delegates embodied their ideas in the constitution.
Embroil in	Ram refused to become embroiled in the argument.
Emigrate from	The starving peasants emigrated from their country.
Empty of	This paragraph is completely empty of meaning.
Enamored of	Pygmalion became enamored of his statue.

Encompass by	The field was encompassed by a thick forest.
Encroach on (or upon)	I do not intend to encroach upon your jurisdiction.
Endear to	Alok's charm and generosity endear her to everybody.
Endow with by	The college was endowed with a million dollars by Rathi.
Endue with	Children seem to be endued with endless vitality.
Enjoin from	The magistrate enjoined the employer from barring the workers.
Enrich by	A good author enriches his stories with life-like dialogue.
Enthusiastic about (or over)	I can not get enthusiastic over leaving at this time.
Envious of	I am envious of your good fortune.
Envy of	Maria was the envy of all the other students.
Equivalent in	Those two expressions are equivalent in meaning.
Equivalent to	That expression is equivalent to the other.
Esteem for	I have great esteem for that man.
Esteem, in	The people held the president in esteem for his unselfishness.
Estrange from	Dean is estranged from his wife.

Event, in any "whatever happens; in my case"	Tell the truth in any event.
Event, in all "whatever happens"	You should go to class in all events.
Evident in	His guilt is evident in his behavior.
Evident from	It was evident from his question that he was not pleased.
Exact from	Sweta exacted a promise from me not to tell her parents.
Exact in	You should be exact in your spelling.
Excel in	Tony excels in swimming.
Exception to	The word is an exception to the rule.
Excerpt from	The novelist read us an excerpt from his latest book.
Excite about	I did not want to excite you about the fire.
Exclude from	The girls excluded the boy from their conversation.
Exclusive of -	The price is exclusive of the federal taxes.
Exempt from	The teacher exempted Ravi from the examination because of his excellent homework.
Expatiate on	The braggart expatiated on his many talents.

Expend on	The government expended a millions rupees on the dam.
Expressive of	The poem is expressive of Wordsworth's love of nature.
Extricate from	The thief's quick wit extricated him from his predicament.

F

Face to face	I want to discuss his problem with him face to face.
Face up to "acknowledge"	A married man has to face up to his responsibilities.
Face with	The scientist was faced with many unknown.
Factor in	The climate was a factor in our deciding to move to Shimla.
Fall back on "use in an emergency"	You ought to keep that old icebox. You can fall back on it if anything happens to your new refrigerator.
Fall, in (the)	Farmers harvest their crops in the monsoon.
Fall in with "meet by chance"	Punit was killed by the man he had fallen in with at a bar the day before.
Fall into the habit of	Pawan fell into the habit of having a drink before lunch.
Fall off "decrease"	Business in department stores usually falls off in the summer.
Familiar to	That word is not familiar to me.

Familiar with	I am not familiar with that word.
Familiarize with	You should familiarize yourself with those terms so that you can understand your teacher when he uses them.
Fanatic on	Mehra is a fanatic on chess.
Fashion, out of "on longer stylish"	My winter coat is out of fashion.
Fatal to	The operation was fatal to Solanki.
Favour,(in)... of	We are in favour of sending them money right away.
Favour, with	The chairman regarded our proposal with favour.
Fawn on (or upon)	The courtiers fawned on the king.
Fend for	Sameer believes that everybody had to fend for himself in the world.
Ferret out	The detective was able to ferret out the truth.
Figure on	1. "intend" I was figuring on leaving at eight o'clock.
	2. "expect" I was figuring on your support.
Figure out "solve; understand"	That's hard puzzle; I can't figure it out.
Fine for	That tool will be fine for the job.
Finish for	I will finish the work for you.

Fire, by	The forest was destroyed by fire.
Fire, on	Look! That House is on fire.
Fire with	Hemant was fired with the desire to become an actor.
First, at	At first I was nervous, but in a few minutes I felt relaxed.
First, at…glance	At first glance I thought the color was blue, but now I see that it is green.
First, at…sight	I didn't like that man at first sight, and I have not changed my opinion.
First of all "the first of a series; before anything else" (a synonym of first but not of at first)"	First of all, be sure you have the correct kind of paper.
Fix up-	1. "repair" Can you fix my radio up?
	2. "arrange" Please fix your room up in the morning.
	3. "attend to" That dentist will fix your teeth up.
Flat, in no time "quickly; very soon"	Maxie got dressed in no time flat.
Fly into a rage "become very angry"	Suresh flew into a rage when his wife brought her new dress home.

Focus, in	Be sure to get the subject in focus before you snap the camera.
Focus, on	The audience focused its attention on the speaker.
Focus, out of	That picture is unclear because the camera was out of focus.
Forbear from	You should forbear from expressing your feelings publicly.
Foreign to	That idea is completely foreign to my principles.
Fraught with	The expedition into the jungle was fraught with danger.
Fright, in	The girls ran from the snake in fright.
Frighten by	Tanwar was frightened by the tramp.
Frown at	The teacher frowned at the boy making the noise.
Frown on (or upon)	Society frowns on bad manners.
Frugal with	Jimmy has so many responsibilities that he must be careful with his time.
Fun, for "for amusement; without thought of reward"	Abhishek repairs radios for fun.

Fun for the… of it "for amusement; without thought of reward"	Abhishek repairs radios just for the fun of it.
Furnish with	The school does not furnish students with books.
Fuse with	The wire became fused with the heavy load.
Fuss over (or about)	The children fussed about the poor food.
Fuss with	I had a fuss with my wife about money, and she's not speaking to me.

G

Generous about (or in)	Kumar is generous about helping students.
Generous to (or toward or with)	Sahni is generous to his children.
Generous with	Aggarwal is generous with his money.
Get about "circulate, go places"	That old woman certainly gets about.
Get across "make understood"	Have I got that idea across to you?

Get ahead	1. "proceed" I would like to talk about that some more, but we must get ahead with other matters.
	2. "succeed; prosper" You can get ahead only with hard work.
Get ahead of	1. "pass; get in advance of " The car behind wants to get ahead of you.
	2. "surpass; be better than" Manu got ahead of you in that test.
Get along "manage"	If you work hard, you will get along in that job.
Get along in years "grow quite old"	Her grandmother is getting along in years.
Get away (from)	1. "escape" I tried to catch the bird, but it got away.
	2. "leave usually because of unpleasantness" The guard told me to get away from the door.
Get down to "attend seriously to; be specific"	He will tell us to get down to cases.
Get even with " have revenge on"	I'll get even with you for eating my dessert.
Get in the way "be obstructive or annoying"	He was determined to be successful. He was not going to let anything or anybody get in the way.

Get off	1. "make (a joke, sometimes referred to by one)" Sushant got off a good one at the meeting today.
	2. "send; mail" I want to get this package off at once.
Get up	1. "stand up" You should get up when an older person comes in.
	2. " awake, arise; make arise" Sandeepa gets up at 7 a.m., and she gets her children up at 7:30 a.m.
	3. "organize" Ghosh loves to get a committee up.
Gird for "prepare for"	I'm afraid that nation is girding for another war.
Give back (to) "return"	He gave them back to us the next day.
Gladden by	We were all gladdened by the news.
Glance at	Aayush glanced at his watch and announced that the time was up.
Glance, at first	At first glance, the problem seems very difficult.
Glance off	The bullet glanced off a tree and struck Sunny.
Glance through	I was so busy this morning I could only glance through the newspaper.

Glimpse, catch a...of	I caught a glimpse of the Capitol when I passed through Washington on the train.
Gloat over	The miser gloated over his money.
Glory in	There is no glory in self-deception.
Gloss over	Admit your mistake; don't try to gloss it over.
Glow with	That athlete glows with energy.
Go ahead	1. (of) "precede" The band went ahead of the marchers.
	2. (with) "continue" Anurag gave his son permission to go ahead with the plan.
Go along (with)-	1. "accompany" You go along with Amit. I'll come shortly.
	2. "agree" I'll go along with your plan.
Go on	1. "happen" An intellectual man wants to know what is going on in the world.
	2. (an exclamation of disbelief) Go on! You can't make me believe that.
	3. (with) "continue" "Go on," the girl begged when he stopped talking.
	4. (a trip, journey, hike, picnic, outing, vacation, etc.) Basu has gone on a trip and won't be back for a week.

Go through with "complete, bring to an end"	Roy seems very determined about his plan, but I don't think he will go through with it.
Good for	That medicine is good for headaches.
Good, for the…of	You should work harder for your own good.
Good, in… (with)	Joe is in good terms with my mother, she likes him.
Good of	It was good of you to give her my message.
Good with	Coffee is good with biscuits.
Goodness sake, for (a mild exclamation)	For goodness sake, haven't you finished?
Gossip about	Tomar loves to gossip about her neighbours.
Grasp at	A drowning man grasps at straws.
Grasp of	That new student has already got a good grasp of the subject.
Grasp, within one's	The rope was almost within my grasp.
Gratified to	I was gratified to hear the good news.
Gratified with (or at a thing)	The teacher was gratified with the students.
Gratitude to for	The girl showed no gratitude to her benefactor for his help.

Grieve about (or for or over)	Nirmala showed no grief about her husband's death.
Grieve about (or for or over)	For the rest of his life, Mihir grieved about the loss of his child.
Grind out "produce mechanically"	That author grinds a novel out every six months.
Grumble about (or at)	Students often grumble about their massive homework.
Guard against	You should guard against catching a cold.
Guess, by	Don't make a cake by guess.

H

Habit of	Raman has the habit of biting his finger nails.
Habitual with	Honesty should be habitual with you.
Haggle with over (or about)	I haggled with the seller over the price.
Hand in "give, submit"	Please hand your homework in at once.
Hand, off (usually written together, offhand) "without prior or full thought"	Offhand, I can't remember where he lives.

Hang around (or about) "loiter in the vicinity of"-	Young men often hang around a women's college.
Hang, get the… of "learn the precise manner or meaning of"-	A young bride has to get the hang of cooking.
Hang out	1. "suspend" On Republic Day people hang flags out. 2. "frequent" Young men sometimes hang out at pool rooms.
Hang up "put the phone on the hook or in the cradle: terminate a call"	Sally hung up before I had a chance to explain.
Health, in good (or bad or poor)	Kapoor is finally in good health again.
Heaps of "much; many"-	Goswami has heaps of work.
Heartless to	Arjun was heartless to desert his family.
Heedless of	The driver was heedless of the warning the policeman had given him.
Hinder from—by	His wife's arrival hindered Ritesh from leaving.
Hint at	He hinted at where we might find the answer.

Hit it off (with) "be agreeable; like"	Ashmit and Rishant hit it off the first time they met.
Hit on (or upon) "find, devise"	Rahul hit on a way to increase his business.
Hold down	1. "suppress, restrain" When Rahul gets mad, you can't hold him down.
	2. "keep (a job)" Satyam seems to be unable to hold any job down.
Hold in "repress, restrain"	I was so irritated I could not hold my anger in.
Hold off -	1. "abstain, keep (from doing)" The rain may hold off for a while.
	2. "be aloof" Goyal holds off from everybody. I think he is shy.
Hold on	1. "wait" When I telephoned, his secretary asked me to hold on.
	2. "grasp" When you're standing in the subway, you'd better hold on to the strap.
Hold out	1. "last" The enemy will surrender because their supplies won't hold out.
	2. "continue to resist or endure" The enemy will not hold out much longer.
Homesick for	Do you feel homesick for your native country?

Hostile to (or toward)	At first, the Indians were not hostile to the explorers.
Hour, on the "at one (or two, etc.) o'clock exactly"	The station broadcasts the news every hour on the hour.
House, on the "free"	After four drinks, the bar gives you one on the house.
Hunger for	The hermit's hunger for fresh fruit led him back to the town.
Hungry for	I am hungry for a good lunch.
Hunt for	The police are making a hunt for the fugitive.

I

Identical with	This paper is identical with that.
Identify by	Sohan identified his watch by the scratch on the case.
Identify with	Einstein is identified with higher mathematics.
Imbue with	The coach imbued the players with a sense of team work.
Immigrate to from	A number of refugees immigrated to this country from Bangladesh.
Immerse in	The boy was immersed in his books.
Impart to	The lawyer imparted the secret to me.
Impassive to	The tyrant was impassive to the mother's plea.

Impatient to	The horse was impatient to start the race.
Impatient with	You should not be impatient with old people.
Implicit in	A warning was implicit in his words.
Impose on (or upon)	A government should justify all restrictions imposed on its citizens.
Impress with	I wish to impress you with the necessity of studying.
Impress by	I was impressed by the beauty of the scene.
Impress on	I wish to impress on you that you must study.
Impression of	In that household I get the impression of being in a dungeon.
Impression on (or upon)	Many novels leave no impression on their readers.
Impression, under the	I was under the impression that you were coming at one o'clock.
Improvement in	You are showing great improvement in your spelling.
Improvement on	The second edition certainly is an improvement on the first.
Incapable of	Rawat seems to be incapable of keeping a job.
Incentive to	Payment is an incentive to effort.
Inclination to (or toward)	I have an inclination to stay here.

Incline to	Your offer inclines me to accept the position.
Incompatible with	Lawlessness is incompatible with civilization.
Incomprehensible to	His statement was completely incomprehensible to me.
Incongruous with	Such a theory is incongruous with the facts.
Inconsiderate of	You should never be inconsiderate of other people's feelings.
Inconsistent in	Yadav is sometimes inconsistent in his statements.
Inconsistent with	Singh's first statement was inconsistent with his second.
Incorporate in	The president's suggestion was incorporated in the new law.
Increase from—to	I increased his salary from Rs.16000 to Rs.18000.
Increase in	There has been an increase in crime lately.
Incumbent on (or upon)	I felt it was incumbent on me to give her an explanation.
Indict for	The suspect was indicted for the crime of manslaughter.
Indispensable to (or for)	Training is indispensable to a doctor.
Indulgent to	Ranbir is too indulgent to his children.

Infect with	Mosquitoes infect human beings with malaria.
Inferior to	A henpecked husband acts inferior to his wife.
Infer from	I infer from your statement that you are not willing to agree.
Infest with	Kitchens may become infested with cockroaches.
Inflict on (or upon)	I don't want to inflict my troubles on you.
Inflict with	I don't want to inflict you with my troubles
Infringe on (or upon)	I have no desire to infringe on your authority.
Infuse with	The news infused the girl with happiness.
Inherent in	The urge to survive is inherent in all creatures.
Inherit from	I inherited my blue eyes from my mother.
Inhibit from	His training inhibited him from expressing his thoughts.
Inimical to	Shyam has always seemed inimical to his uncle.
Initiate into	The members initiated Paul into the fraternity last night.
Inquire into	Let's inquire into that matter a little more.

Inquire of about	I inquired of my cousin about the arrangement.
Insert in (or into)	You can insert additional pages into that book.
Insist on (or upon)	The farmer insisted on his rights.
Inspire by with	The men were inspired by their leader's words with new hope.
Inspire to	His kindness inspired me to write a poem.
Instance, for	We have some Oriental words in English, for instance, *kimono*.
Instance, in this (or that)	In this instance we have an example of modification.
Instant, at that	The door bell rang at that night.
Instigate against	The plotters instigated a revolt against the government.
Instill in (or into)	His father instilled a fear of failure in Lemuel.
Insure against –for with	Bhavesh insured his house against fire for fifteen thousand rupees with the company.
Intent on (or upon)	That politician is intent on changing the regulations.
Intercede with – for	The committee interceded with the judge for the boy.
Interfere with	I wish you would not interfere with my plans.

Interference with	Anuj will not tolerate interference with his direction.
Interpolate in	Mary interpolated a remark in our conversation.
Interrupt in – by	Mohan was interrupted in his speech by applause.
Intervene in	The teacher intervened in the students' argument.
Intrigue with (or by)	I was intrigued with his unusual speech.
Intrude on (or upon)	A stranger intruded on our conversation.
Invest in	You should invest your money in that new company.
Irritate by	I was irritated by his remark.
Isolate from	No country can isolated itself from international problems.
Issue, at "under discussion"	That is the point at issue right now.

J

Jack up "lift; increase"	The mechanic jacked the car up to repair the tire.
Jam, in a "in trouble"	Sanford got in a jam when he left without permission.
Jam with	The train station was jammed with travellers.
Jar on	The unpleasant music jarred on my nerves.

Jeer at	The spectators jeered at the unpopular player.
Jeopardy, in	Dutt put his life in jeopardy to save the drowning child.
Jest, in	Don't get angry; I said that in jest.
Jiffy, in a "quickly; very soon"	The mechanic repaired the machine in a jiffy.
Joy in	The minister wished the couple joy in their marriage.
Judge between "make a choice between"	You must judge between those two applicants.
Judge by (or from)	You should not judge a man by his clothes.
Jump to a conclusion "make a deduction too hastily"	Mildred jumped to the conclusion that Jim loved her just because he was polite to her.
Justify to – by	Karan tried to justify his action to me by saying that he was late.

K

Keen about	Rahul is very keen about soccer.
Keep away (from) "not go near"	Keep away from that animal; it is dangerous.
Keep from "restrain from"	It is too bad that the rain kept you from going to the party.

Knack for	Khanna has the knack for saying the right thing at the right time.
Knock off	1. "stop (especially with work)" The builders knocked off at five o'clock.
	2. "dispose of; get rid of" Let's knock this problem off and go ahead.
Knock out "make unconscious or stop functioning"	The boxer knocked his opponent out.
Knowledge of	Sandeepa has no knowledge of Sanskrit.
Knowledge, to one's "as far as I know"	To my knowledge, the boy did the work alone.
Knuckle down (to) "apply oneself earnestly (to)"	If you want to pass, you'd better knuckle down to your studies.

L

Lack, (for)...of	For lack of something else to do, we went to the movies.
Lapse into	Amar lapses into his native dialect when he returns home.
Large, at	1. "without confinement" There are a number of criminals at large.

	2. "without restraint; at length" Ankit tends to speak at large about his speciality.
	3. "in general; altogether" People at large are not bad creatures.
Large, by and "in general; usually"	By an large, legal proceedings work reasonably well.
Leaf through	The student leafed through his new textbook with interest.
Lean on (or against)	Please don't lean on my chair.
Lecture on (or about)	Professor Hussain lectured on history yesterday.
Leisure, at	1. "not busy; not employed" I'll be at leisure tomorrow; I'll talk with you then.
	2. "without haste" Vajpayee is methodical and slow: he does everything at leisure.
Lenient with (or on) – about	Kashyap is too lenient with his children about their bad manners.
Let down "disappoint; fail"	You let me down when you didn't win the prize.
Level at (or on)	Jay leveled his gaze on me.
Level with	Please level the picture with the table.
Liable to – for	The clerks are liable to the supervisor for their conduct.

Liberal with	Kartik is liberal with his time and money.
Liberty, at	I am not at liberty to discuss that confidential matter.
Lie on	The ill woman was lying on the couch in the living room.
Life, for "for the duration of one's life"	The criminal was sentenced to prison for life.
Lightning, by	The tree was struck by lightning.
Likeness to	People have often commented on his likeness to his father.
Limit to	There is no limit to that child's imagination.
Little by little "gradually"	If you keep practicing, your ability will improve little by little.
Live in (a room, house, apartment, city, state, country, or continent)	Are you living in an apartment?
Live on	1. (a street) - I live on Claremont Avenue.
	2. "feed on; rely on for maintenance" We live on what we eat.
	3. "continue to exist" After his severe accident, Prakash lived on for several years.

Long, before	Keep trying, and, before long, you will speak English very well.
Long, so (or as)...as "if"	You may borrow my book so long as you promise to return it tomorrow.
Look ahead "plan for the future"	A wise man always looks ahead.
Look around "search, but not intently"	When you want to rent a house, you should look around at first.
Look away "turn one's eyes aside"	When I glanced at the nurse, she looked away.
Look into "investigate"	The police are looking into the numerous fires that have occurred recently.
Look over "examine"	Sanju's mother looked his letter over before he mailed it.
Look through	1. "examine" I looked through the newspaper, but I could not find any report on the accident. 2. "look at without appearing to recognize" When I passed Pooja this morning, she looked straight through me.
Look to for "expect from"	You must look to your father for help.
Loyal to	That boy is always loyal to his friends.

Lucky to	You are lucky to be alive.

M

Make a fuss about (or over)	Those old men are making a fuss over that young man again.
Make for "try to reach"	We'd better make for home before it starts to rain.
Make fun of "ridicule"	The little boys made fun of Sunny's haircut.
Make over "show affectionate admiration for"	Most women make over a baby whenever they see one.
Make up to "try to become friendly with; flatter"	Some students make up to their teachers in hopes of getting a good grade.
Mania for	Constance has a mania for keeping everything neat.
Mark down "reduce the price of"	The store has marked its summer dresses down.
Mark off for "reduce a grade or score because of"	I will mark off for misspellings.
Marvel at	I marveled at the acrobat's daring.
Match for...in	The challenger was no match for the champion in skill.

Means, by all "certainly; of course (an intensifier)"	By all means, invite Sohail to the party if you want to.
Means, by no "not at all; absolutely not"	I am by no means pleased at your answer.
Means, by...of "with the help of"	He gained his supremacy by means of bribery.
Means of	Rastogi has no means of supporting herself.
Meantime, in the	I will leave for Europe next week. In the meantime I've got to pack.
Meanwhile, in the	Bert will arrive tonight. In the meanwhile you should get his room ready.
Mend, on the "recovering; recuperating"	Henna was very sick, but he's on the mend now.
Midst, in the...of	Saingar was interrupted in the midst of his speech.
Migrate between	Many birds migrate between the northern and the southern hemisphere.
Migrate from – to	The Pilgrims migrated from England to America.

Mind, keep (or bear) in "remember"	Keep that rule in mind.
Mind, in	I have a good example in mind.
Mind, in one's right "sane"	Komal was not in her right mind when she accused the boy.
Mind, make up one's	Make your mind up whether you are going with us or not.
Mind, out of one's "insane"	Joe was out of his mind when he made that suggestion.
Mingle with	The townspeople did not mingle with the newcomers at first.
Model on	The author modelled the character on a well known phonetician.
Monopoly in	That company has a monopoly in copper.
Multiply by	If you multiply four by two, you get eight.
Muse on (or upon)	I mused on the contents of the letter.
Muster up "gather"	I had to muster my courage up to ask him that question.

N

Name after "give the same name as"	I was named after my father.

Necessary for (or to.) A following infinitive has *to*; the subject of that infinitive has *for*)	Food is necessary for life. Food is necessary to life. It is necessary to eat. It is necessary for us to live.
Necessity for	Inventions create a necessity for new terms.
Necessity, of "inevitably; unavoidably"	A rhetorician of necessity deals with attitudes.
News to	The committee took the news to the mayor.
Next to	Next to apply pie, my favorite dessert is strawberry shortcake.
Nice to	A hostess is expected to be nice to all her guests.
Noon, at	The whistle blows at noon.
North of	Boston is north of New York.
North, to the…of	Boston is to the north of New York.
Noted for	Greece is noted for its beautiful islands.
Nothing, for	1. "uselessly" I did all that work for nothing. It was all wrong. 2. "without cost" I got a second pair of trousers for nothing when I bought the suit.

Nothing, in…flat "very quickly"	My wife can fix dinner in nothing flat.
Nothing to say…of "not to mention"	I am having a hard time with biology, to say nothing of physics.

O

Obedient to	Children should be obedient to their parents.
Object to	I object to that kind of talk.
Obliged to	for I am obliged to leave in a few minutes.
Obtain from	You can obtain the application form from the registrar.
Occasion for	Samar's arrival was an occasion for celebrating.
Occasion, on "now and then; occasionally"	I am not much of a movie fan, but I do go to the movies on occasion.
Occur to	A horrible accident has occured to Sahil.
Offensive to	That boy's carelessness is offensive to a neat person.
Once and for all, (for) "definitively; now but never again"	I will answer your question for once and for all.
Open to	The meeting is open to everybody.

Opinion on (or about)	I expressed my opinion on the political situation.
Opposed to	I am opposed to changing the plans.
Opposite of, the	Samir's reply was just the opposite of what I had expected.
Optimistic about	Priya is very optimistic about winning the scholarship.
Option on	The movie company took an option on Winwar's book.
Outlook on	Bharti's outlook on life is very optimistic.
Over and above " in addition to; besides"	What are your expenditures over and above those for board and room?
Over and over (again) "repeatedly"	I have told you over and over again that I did not do that.

P

Parallel to (or with)	That line is parallel to the lower line.
Part with "relinquish"	No, I don't want to sell my car. I don't want to part with it.
Partial to	A parent should not show preference by being partial to one child.
Participate in	Bobby would not participate in the other children's games.
Particular about	Thompson is very particular about his clothes.

Particular, in	I have nothing in particular to add to what he said.
Pass over " disregard"	If you don't know the answer to the second question, just pass it over.
Patience with	You should have patience with children.
Patient with	You should be patient with children.
Pep up "enliven; give vigour or spirit to"	The coach's talk pepped the boys up.
Perfect for	It is a perfect day for a picnic.
Perk up "become or make lively"	Sarah perked up shortly after her illness.
Pertain to	The lawyer produced documents pertaining to the case.
Phone, by	Gigoo made the final arrangements by phone.
Phone, on (or over) the	Gigoo made the final arrangements on the phone.
Pine for	Anurag is homesick: he's pining for his mother's cooking.
Pity for	I felt pity for the helpless child.
Place for	The company found a place for the unemployed man.
Place, in "in the proper location"	The maid will put the furniture in place.
Plan for	You should always plan for the future.

Plan on	You must plan on spending at least ten dollars for a room in that hotel.
Play on (or upon) appeal to (one's feelings) for a favour"	I see that Bobby got what he wanted. He must have played upon your sympathy.
Play out	1. "become or make exhausted" The ore in that mine has played out. 2. "finish" Let's play this game out.
Play up "give importance or publicity to"	The newspapers played the event up.
Plead with	I pleaded with my mother to let me go.
Pleasant to	A clerk should be pleasant to customers.
Pleased at (or about or with)	I am not pleased with your attitude.
Pleasure of	I have had the pleasure of meeting your mother.
Plenty of	You have plenty of time to finish your examination.
Polish up "improve"	You'd better polish your French up before you go to Paris.
Poor in	A desert is poor in vegetation.
Popular with	Ravikant is very popular with his students.

Positive of (or about)	Are you positive of that?
Possession, in...of	The murderer was not in possession of all his senses.
Possibility for	There is always a possibility of doing it another way.
Possible for	It is not possible for me to go to the movies tonight.
Pounce on (or upon)	The cat pounced on the mouse.
Practice, in	Vinay is full of suggestions that are not good in practice.
Praise, in...of	The young man wrote a poem in praise of his sweetheart.
Pray to – for	The tribe prayed to its gods for rain.
Precious to	My child is precious to me.
Preface to	You should always read the preface to a book.
Preferable to	I think the blue dress is preferable to the green one.
Prejudice against	An ignorant person has prejudice.
Preliminary to	We'd better have a talk preliminary to the full meeting.
Preparation for	Have you made any preparation for your trip?
Presence, in the...of	I wish you would not say such things in my presence.

Present with	The committee presented Kunal with an award with efforts.
Preserve for	You should preserve your papers for future use.
Preside over	Hari presided over the meeting.
Prevent from	Abhinav's injury does not prevent him from enjoying life.
Prevention against	Times installed a lock as a prevention against theft.
Previous to	Previous to her marriage, her name was Clark.
Price, at any	Arvind was determined to succeed at any price.
Prior to	Prior to graduating, a student must take a comprehensive examination.
Priority over	Nikhil has priority over you: he has been here longer.
Proceeds from	The proceeds from the sale were used for scholarship.
Proficient in	Are you proficient in English?
Prohibit from	There is a law prohibiting people from smoking in the subway.
Prominent in	Sagar is prominent in politics.
Prone to	Sekhar is prone to anger.
Proof against	That man is guilty. The police have a lot of proof against him.
Proof of	The police have proof of that man's guilty.

Protect from	An umbrella will protect you from the rain.
Protest against	I will make a protest against the rulling.
Proud of (or about)	Mark is proud of his new son. He was proud about getting a first class.
Prove to	You will have to prove to me that you are really a serious student.
Provide for	You should provide for your old age.
Provide with	The hostess provided us with blankets.
Provision for	You should make provision for your old age.
Provoke to	Her carelessness provoked him to speak in anger.
Punishment for	Rajan received punishment for what he had done.
Purchase from	I purchased the carving from a well-known artist.
Put through	1. " make (a telephone call)"Rakesh put a call through to his wife. 2. "pass (a law or regulation)" Congress has put through a law raising taxes.

Q

Qualification for	The applicant has all the qualifications for the job.

Qualify for	Your score qualifies you for the next class.
Question (noun) of (or about)	There is no question of his honesty. He is reliable.
Quick to	Praveen was quick to deny the accusation.

R

Rage about (or over)	Sehgal raged about the high prices.
Range from – to	Those dresses range in price from eighteen to fifty dollars.
Rate, at any	1. "at all events; nevertheless" At any rate, you must go to class.
	2. "at least" Sunita is very rich; at any rate, she spends a lot of money.
Reach for	The policeman reached for his gun, but he was too slow.
Reach, out of	You must keep poisons out of reach of children.
Reach, within	Old Mahesvari kept her cane within reach.
React to	How did your mother react to your news?
Read about (or of)	Did you read about the President's sickness?
Read to	Did your mother read to you when you were a child?

Read up on "become informed about by reading"	You had better read up on French before you take your psychology examination.
Reason for	My teacher gave me several reasons for studying harder.
Reason with	You can't reason with that man: he's stubborn.
Rebel against	This language always rebels against my attempt to master it.
Recall to	Tyagi recalled to her husband that he had told her the story before.
Reckon with	You will have to reckon with your landlord about getting your apartment painted.
Recommend to – for	Which material did the salesgirl recommend to you for the dress?
Reconcile to	The criminal became reconciled to his fate.
Recover from	Have you recovered from your illness?
Recuperate from	Benson is still recuperating from his operation.
Refer to	You should refer to your dictionary when you are not sure about a word.
Reference to, (in)	I have nothing to say in reference to that incident.
Reflect on (or upon)	The sunlight reflected on the wall.

Refrain from	The nurse asked me to refrain from smoking in the room.
Regard as	I regard Walter as my best friend.
Regard for	Potter is very selfish: he has no regard for anyone else.
Regard to, in	In regard to your last question, I will make this statement.
Register for	Bert registered for a course in economics.
Reign over	Silence reigned over the crowd.
Relate to	The teacher related the incident to his previous lecture.
Relative to	The discussion was relative to the future growth of the company.
Release from	The innocent man was released from jail.
Rely on (or upon)	You can rely on me for help.
Remark on (or upon or about)	The teacher remarked on your absence yesterday.
Remedy for	That tablet is a good remedy for headaches.
Remove from	The doctor removed the girl from the crowded room.
Renowned for	Einstein is renowned for his work in mathematics.
Reply, in…to	What did you say in reply to the boy's question?

Report (noun) on (or about)	Jitendra made a report on the company's activities to the stockholders.
Request (noun) for	The soldier made a request for a transfer to another post.
Resemblance between	There is a strong resemblance between Kapoor and his son.
Resemblance to	Surendar has a great resemblance to his father.
Resort to	The policeman had to resort to force when the thief refused to surrender.
Respects, in all	Ashish resembles his father in all respects.
Respond to	The lecturer kindly respond to my question.
Response from—on (or to or about)	Have you received a response from the school on your application?
Restrain from	I had to restrain myself from making an unkind remark.
Result (verb) in	Geeta carelessness resulted in an accident.
Result (noun) of	The accident was the result of Geeta carelessness.
Retire from	The applicant retired from the room after the interview.
Return, in...for	I gave Kunal some books in return for his assistance.

Return to—from	I am going to return to my country in a few months.
Reveal to	Tabassum revealed her secret to her husband.
Revenge on (or upon)—for	Bhawna got revenge on her attacker.
Revert to	The conversation reverted to the original topic.
Rich in	Italy is rich in skilled workers.
Right in	You were right in your answer.
Ring off "end a telephone call"	I must ring off now.
Ring up "telephone"	I'm going to ring Nupur up.
Ripe for	That apple is ripe for eating.
Rise against	The peasants rose against the tyrant.
Rise from	The sick man rose from his chair and walked to the door.
Rival in	Nobody can rival Newsome in gossiping.
Road, on the "travelling"	The theatrical company spent six months on the road.
Root in	The plants were rooted in fertile ground.
Rope in "capture; entice"	That girl certainly roped you in with her charm.
Round up "gather"	Let's round up the gang and go on a picnic.

Rule, as a (general) "generally"	As a rule, proper names do not have an article.
Rule on "make a decision about"	The judge will rule on the controversy.
Run after	The policeman ran after the thief.
Run against "be the opponent of in an election"	Roosevelt ran against Hoover in 1932.
Run off "make copies of"	The publishers ran off a thousand copies of his book.
Run out (of) "exhaust the supply (of)"	I can't make a cake; I've run out of sugar.
Run out (on) "desert"	Don't run out on your friends when they need you.
Run through	1. "look at, read, or say quickly" The teacher ran through his papers to see if he had mine.
	2. "consume rapidly" Our boy can run through his clothes quicker than we can buy them.
Run to "total"	The books runs to 245 pages.
Rush, in a	I can't talk to you now; I'm in a rush.

S

Sacred to	Cows are sacred to certain religious groups.
Sacrifice to	Jeet sacrificed everything to his ambition.

Saddle with	Yogendra saddled his partner with the blame.
Satisfaction in	Eliyaj finds satisfaction in his job.
Satisfaction with	My boss showed his satisfaction with my work.
Satisfactory for	The house is no longer satisfactory for our needs.
Scare of	Are you scared of horses?
Scare off "make leave through fright"	The girl's screams scared the man off.
Scare up " get, usually with difficulty"	I've got to scare some money up for my rent.
Schedule, off "unpunctual; either later or earlier than planned; not at the stage of development planned or expected"	We must do the parts of the project in order. If we do get off schedule in one part, we will get confused in the other parts.
Schedule, on "punctual; at the expected time"	If my train is on schedule, I will be home by nine o'clock.
Scrape up "collect, usually with difficulty"	I must scrape up some money for tuition.

Scratch, from "from the beginning; from nothing"	Now, repeat the poem from scratch.
Screw up "muster, gather" (usually with courage or nerve)	I finally screwed up enough courage to ask for a raise.
Sea, at	1. "on the ocean"
	2. "confused; unable to under-stood" I felt completely at sea when I first arrived in this country.
Secede from	The state seceded from the union in 1998.
Secure from	Most people want to be secure from financial worry.
Sell for "sell at the price of"	Mayank sold the car for 50 thousand rupees.
Sequel to	Have you read the sequel to Hiram's novel?
Sequence, in	You must take those courses in sequence, not simultaneously.
Set about "start"	The maid set about cleaning the room.
Set against	Mohan is completely set against our proposal, and we can't change his mind.

Set aside "defer; reserve"	We will set discussion of that aside until tomorrow.
Set on fire	The arsonist set several houses on fire.
Settle down "become serious-minded"	Most men settle down after they get married.
Settle for	The plaintiff settled his claim for a thousand dollars.
Settle up "pay (a bull)"	Let's settle up and leave this restaurant.
Sever from	The ax blow severed the bough from the tree.
Shake hands with	Men customarily shake hands with each other when they are introduced.
Shame for	Edward shows no shame for his laziness.
Shame, put to "disgrace; surpass"	That studious boy puts his lazy brother to shame.
Shoot up "grow rapidly"	Pratap's boy has shot up in the last two years.
Shoulder, straight from the "without evasion"	I will give you my opinion straight from the shoulder.
Shout at	Please don't shout at me; I can hear.

Shout for	The drowning man shouted for help.
Shrink from	The girl shrank from the repulsive sight.
Shudder at	I shudder at the thought of the child's dying.
Shy at	The horse shied at the strange object in the road.
Sick of "tired of"	I am sick of your excuses.
Side against "be opposed to, along with someone else"	My father always sides against me when my brother and I argue.
Sidewalk, on the	I found a rupee on the sidewalk yesterday.
Sit on (a chair with one or two arms)	My grandmother used to sit in her rocking chair for hours.
Sit up	1. "sit erect" Sit up; don't slouch in your seat.
	2. "stay out of bed" Tandan sat up all night because her child was sick.
Skeptical of (or about)	I am skeptical of that statement.
Skill in	Khosla is skilled in surgery.
Skillful in (or at)	That carpenter is skillful in his work.

Slack off "become less active"	Business slacks off during the summer.
Slide on	The car slid on the wet pavement.
Slip up "make a mistake"	The murderer slipped up when he left his finger prints on the weapon.
Slow down "decrease speed (of)"	Slow down before you get to that curve.
Smack of	Henry's story smacks of a vivid imagination.
Smart to	You were smart to reject his offer.
Smell of	The lady's clothes smelled of roses.
Smile at	The old lady smiled at me very kindly.
Snap at	My dog always snaps at strangers.
Snap off "stop the operation of (an appliance)"	Bob snapped off the light when he left the kitchen.
Snap on "begin the operation of (an appliance)"	Snap the fan on; it's hot in here.
Sneer at	The manager sneered at my suggestion.
Solution to	Marriage is considered to be a solution to loneliness.
Sorry for	Ankit felt sorry for the blind man.
Sorry to	I am sorry to hear you say that.
Speak to—about	Did you speak to your boss about a raise?

Speak, to…of "worth mentioning; very little"	Vijay has no money to speak of.
Specific in	Please be specific in your answers.
Spirits, in good (or bad)	Sandu is very cheerful. He is always in good spirits.
Spite, in…of	Harsh went to school in spite of his illness.
Spiteful to	Sally was spiteful to the man who had helped her.
Spring at	The tiger sprang at the hunter.
Spur on "incite; encourage"	John's ambition spurs him on.
Spur, on the…of the moment "suddenly; without much prior thought"	He did it on the spur of the moment.
Square with	I am square with my doctor since I have paid my bill.
Stack of "much; many"	I've got a stack of work to do.
Stake, at	Your reputation is at stake.
Stand by	1. "aid; support" No matter what happens, I will stand by you. 2. "wait; be prepared" Would you stand by for a few minutes?
Stand off	1. "hold at a distance" The soldiers stood the attackers off for several hours.

	2. "be unsociable" Hooper stands off even at a party.
Stand on (or upon)	1. "depend on" I depend on you.
	2. "be strict about observing (formality, one's rights, etc.) You must act respectful to him; he stands upon ceremony.
Stare at	It is impolite to stare at people.
Start off "begin"-	The speaker started off with an anecdote.
Start with	I want everybody to recite; I'll start with Karan.
Stealth, by	The money was removed from the vault by stealth.
Stem from	Those two men's enmity stems from their rivalry in high school.
Step up "increase"	The police are stepping up their compaign against drugs.
Stick around "stay near"	Stick around until I finish.
Stick to "persevere in"	Rangnathan finishes a job because he sticks to it.
Stir up "arouse, excite"	Don't stir the children up with that story.
Stoop to	I never thought you would stoop to such ungentlemanly behavior.

Straighten out	1. "clarify; resolve" Mann and Jeet had an argument, but they finally straightened out their differences.
	2. "make (a person) understand" I could not grasp the theory until Rose straightened me out on it.
Straighten up "makes neat or orderly	I have got to straighten my room up.
Stricken with	The union has called a strike against that company.
Strike, on	The workers have been on strike for a week.
Strip from	His clothing was stripped from the baby.
Strive after (or for)	An intellectual strives after knowledge.
Strive against	Hercules strove against his enemies.
Stuck up "conceited"	Miss Lee is stuck up about her appearance.
Style, in "fashionable"	A well- tailored suit is always in style.
Style, out of "old- faishioned; no longer modish"	The Charleston is out of style.
Subject to	The prisoners was subjected to torture.

Submit to	Have you submitted your application to the consulate?
Subordinate to	You must subordinate your desires to the good of the community.
Subscribe to	I have subscribed to that magazine for years.
Subsist on	Squirrels subsist on nuts during the winter.
Substitute for	The thief substituted his imitation for the real painting.
Subtract from	If you subtract three from seven, you get four.
Subway, by	Do you come to class by subway?
Subway, on the	Do you come to class on the subway?
Succession, in	Bobby ate three hamburgers in succession.
Sue for	The plaintiff sued the company for damage to his property?
Sufficient for	I have saved an amount sufficient for a week's vacation.
Suit to	Epson suited his speech to the occasion.
Sum up "summarize"	The chairman summed the discussion up in a few words.
Summer time, in (the)	New York gets very hot in the summer time.
Superior to	A conceited man feels superior to everyone else.

Superiority over	That boy shows superiority over his brother.
Superstitious about	Are you superstitious about black cats?
Supplement by	Paul supplement his income by working part-time.
Supremacy over	We are trying to gain supremacy over our opponents.
Surpass in	Nicholas surpasses his brother in intelligence.
Sweat it out "wait nervously"	You will hear about your exam grade tomorrow. In the mean time you will have to sweat it out.
Swing, in full	The party was in full swing by nine o'clock: everybody was having a fine time.
Sympathize with—about (or on)	I sympathize with you.
Sympathy for	Brown expressed his sympathy for the unfortunate child.

T

Tabs on "knowledge or account of"	Anita's baby is so active that it is hard for her to keep tabs on him.
Take back "surprise; confuse"	Philip's reply took me aback.
Take back	1. "return" You should take those books back to library.

	2. "retract; apologize for" If you don't take back what you just said, Lucy will slap you.
Take down "write; record"	You had better take my address down.
Take hold of	1. " seize" Take hold of that end, and help me move this table.
	2. "become popular with" That fad has taken hold of teen-agers.
Take in	1. " include" There are a lot of sights you ought to see. That tour takes them in.
	2. "deceive" Oh, that magician didn't take me in. I knew it was a trick.
	3. "make smaller" After her illness, Jay had to take all her dresses in.
Take off	1. "remove (used with clothes)" Take your hat off.
	2. "leave the ground (used with planes) The plane took off very smoothly.
Take on "undertake to do"	I'll take that assignment on.
Take out "remove; delete"	Don't keep your hand in your pockets; take them out.

Take over "assume control or direction (of)"	When the new manager took over the store, he made it more efficient.
Take stock of "consider; evaluate"	You should take stock of your abilities.
Take up "tighten"	You had better take that screw up; it is getting loose.
Talent for	Robin has no talent for singing.
Talk back (to) "answer impolitely"	You should not talk back to your mother.
Talk into "persuade"	Phil talked me into going with him.
Talk out of	1. "dissuade" My wife talked me out of buying a new car. 2. "get from by talking" The beggar talked me out of me a dollar.
Talk over "discussed at length, often for the purpose of making a decision"	We had better talk the matter over before we take a vote.
Tally with	Luke's version of the accident does not tally with mine.
Tantamount to	Lyson's statement was tantamount to a confession.
Taste in "judgment of"	Alice's taste in clothes is excellent.

Taste, in good (or bad or poor)	Your joke was in bad taste.
Tax on	You have to pay a sales tax on everything you buy in New York City.
Tear down "demolish"	Wreckers will tear that old building down soon.
Tear into "attack with vigour"	The professor tore into my statement.
Tease about	My grandchildren tease about how old-fashioned people were in my youth.
Television, on	Did you see Sushant on television last night?
Tendency toward	That novelist has a tendency toward wordiness.
Thank for	I thank you for your advice.
Thanks, give… for	We gave Johnson our thanks for helping us.
Think to oneself "think but not say aloud"	Ellen thought to herself that her father was wrong.
Threaten with	The czar threatened the spy with death.
Thrive on	Plants thrive on sunshine and water.
Throw at "throw with the intention to hit"	The boy threw a stone at the dog.

Throw away "discard; not take"	I ought to throw this hat away.
Throw to "throw in order to be caught"	Throw the ball to me.
Throw up "abandon"	I'm ready to throw my job up.
Tie up	The clerk tied the package up for me.
Time, at the right	The truly wise man knows how to do the right thing at the at the right time.
Time, at the same	I want to increase my knowledge, but at the same time I am lazy.
Time, for the…being "temporarily"	For the time being, we can use this tool.
Time, in due	Don't get impatient; you will be told in due time.
Time, in no… (flat) "quickly; very soon"	Casey started working for the company, and in no time he received two promotions.
Time off " period away from regular work"	I'm going to Goa when I have some time off.
Time out "suspension of action"	One team asked for time out to discuss a plan.

Timid about	Jolson is timid about expressing his opinion.
Tip off "inform secretly"	The girl tipped Jim off that the police wanted him.
Tired from "physically exhausted from"	Nelson is tired from working hard today.
Tired off "emotionally weary of"	I am tired of cold weather.
Tired out "completely exhausted"	Tolson was tired out after his long walk.
Touch at " stop briefly at"	Our ship touched at Charleston for a few hours.
Touch, in...with	Do you keep in touch with your old friends?
Touch on (or upon) "speak or write briefly about"	The lecturer touched on Kashmir in his talk.
Touch up "modify; improve"	The artist touched the house up in the picture.
Toy with	Fisher isn't in town; he went to Thailand last week.
Track of "record or knowledge of"	Do you keep track of all your expenditures?
Train, by	Perkins went to Georgia on a train.
Trample on (or upon)	The football players trampled on the grass.

Transfer to—from	We frequently want to transfer ourselves to another century, to another way of life.
Transform into	The countryside was transformed into a huge white plain by the snow.
Translate from—into	Rosa translates her thoughts from Spanish into English.
Trend toward (or to)	Architects have trended toward simplicity in recent years.
Trick into	The widow was tricked into signing the contract.
Trip, on a	Sir has gone on a trip to Honduras.
Triumph over	The girl triumphed over her illness.
Trouble, in	Do you try to help people who are in trouble?
Trouble with	Do you have much trouble with spelling?
Trust in	A gambler puts his trust in luck.
Trust with	I wouldn't trust that bank with my money?
Try for "attempt to get"	I am going to try for prize.
Twilight, at	Bats leave their roosts at twilight.
Typical of	Palm trees are typical of tropical climates.

U

Umbrage, take…at	Carolyn took umbrage at Paul's thoughtless remark.

Unacceptable to	The artist's portrait was unacceptable to the committee.
Unaware of	Arvind was unaware of the mistake he had made.
Uncalled for "inappropriate; in bad taste"	Your remark about Percy's deafness was certainly uncalled for.
Uncertain about	I am uncertain about my future.
Unconscious of	The young boy was unconscious of the mistake he had committed.
Undaunted by	The mountaineer was undaunted by his predecessors' failures.
Unequal to	The country's resources were unequal to the demands of war.
Unequal in	The teams were unequal in skill.
Unfit for	Bose is completely unfit for that job.
Unpopular with	Jay was unpopular with his school mates.
Urge on	My mother urged more food on the young boy.
Useful for	That implement is useful for many purposes in the kitchen.

V

Vacation, on	Dutt won't be in the office for a week; he's on a vacation.
Vain about (or of)	Hilda is very vain about her slender fingers.

Vain, in	I have looked for that book in vain; please help me find it.
Value for	Bose values his secretary for her accuracy.
Variance, (at)…with	My own balance was at variance with the bank's.
Vary from	The educational system in Greece varies from that in Colombia.
Veer from	The ship veered from its course to pick up the survivors of the wreck.
Verge on (or upon)	Your manner verges on impoliteness.
Versed in	Neilson is versed in four languages.
Victim of	I am a victim of circumstances; I can not do anything.
Vie with—for	Polk vied with Matthew for the prize.
View, from a point of	From an artistic point of view, there is nothing remarkable about the scene.
View, in…(of)	The performer stood in view of the spectators.
Virtue, by…of "because of"	That actor achieved his fame by virtue of his skill.
View, with a…to (or toward)	Alec makes friends with a view to using them.
Voice, in a loud (or soft, low, etc.)	A teacher must speak in a loud voice.

Void of	That novel is completely void of merit.
Vouch for	I can vouch for the applicant: I have known him for a long time.
Vote against	Nelson voted against White; he wanted Brown to win.
Vote for	Sandeep voted for the Democratic candidate.
Vote on (a proposal)	Congress will vote on the bill this afternoon.

W

Wager on	Have you made a wager on the contest?
Wait for	We were waiting for a bus.
Wait on (or upon) "serve"	I like salesgirls who wait on me courteously.
Wait up "stay cut of bed"	I will be late tonight. Don't wait up for me.
Walk, go for a	Professor Yadav goes for a walk after dinner.
Warn about (or of)	The teacher warned the boy about coming late to class.
Wartime, in	Certain commodities become scare in wartime.
Wary of	You should be wary of door-to-door salesman.

Watch for	You should watch the newspapers for the announcement of the meeting.
Watch, on the...for	The police are on the watch for pickpockets.
Watch out (for) "be careful (about)"	When you cross the street, watch out for cars.
Wear off "decrease gradually"	You will feel better when the effects of the drug wear off.
Wear out "use until useless"	That child can wear a pair of shoes out in a month.
Will against one's "unwillingly; against one's approval"	The kidnaper took the woman against her will.
Will, at "voluntarily"	We can not stop our heart action at will.
Willing to	I am willing to forget the whole unpleasant incident.
Wind up "excite; make tense"	Continuous arguing always winds me up so that I can not think.
Wonder about	I am wondering about going to a movie tomorrow.
Word of word "literally, exactly"	Abigail repeated the boy's conversation word of word.
Words, in so many	Vernon did not say he did not like Susie in so many words, but that is what he meant.
Work, at	My husband is at work right now.

Work for	Are you working for a Ph.D.?
Work, make short…of "finish or dispose of quickly"	Those farmers made short work of building the new barn.
Work off	1. "fulfil" I had to work off some requirements before I was accepted as a matriculated student. 2. "get rid of" You had better work your anger off before you speak to him.
Work, out of "unemployed"	Whenever my boss sees me out of work, he finds something for me to do.
Work up "prepare; create"	I have to work a programme up for our meeting.
Work with	Kunal is working with Karan on the committee.
Worry about	Robert is worried about his sick mother.
Worse off "in a worse condition"	You should have taken that new job.
Worthy of	That man is worthy of a better job.
Write out "use complete words; do not use abbreviations, figures, or signs"	Don't use abbreviations for and and the United States; write those words out.

| Write up "make a written description or analysis of" | The reporter wrote the accident up for the newspaper. |

Y

| Yearn for | My wife yearns for a home of her own. |
| Yield to | The soldier yielded to the enemy. |

Z

Zeal for	Seth zeal for chess is quite remarkable.
Zeal in	A new secretary usually shows zeal in her work.
Zest for	Ansaari has great zest for outdoor sports.

CONJUNCTION

1. *Both… And, Either… Or, Neither… Nor, Not Only… But* (also). Be careful of false positioning here.

W.	Students must either wear hats or caps.
	He is neither an ascetic in theory nor practice.
	This will not only interest children but also grown-ups.
R.	Students must wear either hats or caps.
	He is an ascetic in neither theory nor practice.
	This will interest not only children but also grown-ups.

| C. | These pairs must be divided with logical precision, the first part always, being followed by the same part of speech as the second part. |

2. *If* and *Whether*. Remember that "if" and "whether" are not always interchangeable.

| W. | Our cat purrs whether you stroke it. |
| | Whether it rains, I shall not come. |

| R. | Our cat purrs if (or whether) you stroke it. |
| | If it rains, I shall not come. |

| C. | "Whether" cannot be used instead of "if" to express a condition or the idea of "whenever". |

3. *Than* and *When*. Distinguish carefully between these two.

| W. | Scarcely had he gone than I remembered his letter. |
| | No sooner had she arrived when the telegram came. |

| R. | Scarcely had he gone when I remembered his letter. |
| | No sooner had she arrived than the telegram came. |

| C. | "Scarcely" is used with "when" . " Than" is use after "else", "other", "otherwise" or the comparative of an adjective or an adverb. |

4. *Than Me* and *Than I*? Remember that "than" is properly a conjunction and should take the same case after it as before it, even when the verb is omitted.

W.	She loves you more than me. (Ambiguous)
R.	She loves you more than I (do).
C.	With transitive verbs "than" must be considered conjunctionally to avoid ambiguity, but modern usage frequently treats "than" prepositionally (with the objective case following it) *when the verb is intransitive, or when the pronoun is qualified by "all or "both".*

e.g. My cousin is younger than me.

She is cleverer than us all.

Her brothers are older than her, but she plays tennis better than them both.

5. *That*. This conjunction must not be misused for "because", "if", "unless", "though".

| W. | If I refuse your invitation, it's not that I don't want to come but because I haven't any time. |
| R. | If I refuse your invitation it's not because I don't want to come but because I haven't any time. |

6. *And That*. Be careful, when using this for introducing a noun clause, to precede it by another noun clause which also begins with "that".

| W. | I felt sure he would die and that his money would go to his son. |
| R. | I felt sure that he would die and that his money would go to his son. |

7. *Try And.* Avoid the conjunction here.

W.	Try and come tomorrow.

R.   Try to come tomorrow.

8. *While and Whilst.* Don't use these conjunctions to mean "and" or "but" or "whereas".

W.	The pundit read the first *mantra* while the bridegroom read the second.
R.	The pundit read the first *mantra* and the bridegroom read the second.
C.	"While" and (less commonly) "whilst" mean "during the time that"

USEFUL IDIOMS

Here are twenty-five of the most important "phrasal verbs" in the language. (Phrasal verbs are verbs followed by prepositions and adverbs which give them special idiomatic meanings).

1. PHRASAL VERB IDIOMS

a) Break

The car broke down (stopped because of a mechanical defect.)

My sister broke down when she heard the bad news (collapsed).

He knows how to break in horses (train, discipline).

Yesterday burglars broke into their house (forced an entry).

A revolution has broken out (begun).

The school breaks up on Thursday (closes for the holidays).

b) Bring

This story brought home to me the seriousness of the situation (made me realize).

You must bring back that book (return)

She fainted, but we brought her round with some brandy (revived).

She has brought up her children very well (reared and educated).

His wonderful speech brought the house down (received great applause).

c) Call

Please call in a doctor at once (ask a doctor to come).

This calls for immediate action (demands, requires)

Shall I call for you at six o'clock (come to collect)?

He called on her this morning (visited).

d) Clear

After breakfast she cleared away (removed dishes etc. from the table).

Clear off! I've had enough of you (go away—colloquial).

They cleared out without paying their rent (departed).

Please clear up your bedroom (make it tidy).

The weather has cleared up at last (brightened).

The lecturer cleared up several points (elucidated, made clear).

e) Come

How did it come about that you went to live in Sri Lanka (happen)?

I came across this book quite by chance (found, discovered).

How did you come by this diamond ring (acquired)?

The price of flour has come down a lot (fallen).

He came into a fortune when his uncle died (inherited).

This book will come in useful (prove useful).

The magazine comes out every Friday (appears).

He split ink on his coat and the stain wouldn't come out (disappear).

He came round quickly after the anaesthetic (returned to consciousness).

How much does the bill come to (total).

The question of higher wages will certainly come up (be raised).

Your work has not come up to standard (reached the required standard).

f) Cut

We really must cut down our expenses (reduce).

He keeps cutting in when I'm talking (interrupting).

His parents cut him off with a shilling (disinherited).

He loves the sea and seems cut out a sailor (fitted, suited to be).

The author cut out all the long words from his book (removed).

Please cut up the meat for the children (cut into small pieces).

He was very cut up about his son's accident (distressed— Always passive).

g) Do

Why don't they do away with all passports (abolish)?

He has a good woman to do for him (do cleaning and cooking for him).

She does out his room thoroughly (clears).

I could do with a drink (would like).

This house needs doing up (repairing and decorating).

Do up your shoe-lace (tie).

h) Draw

Summer is drawing near (approaching).

He drew out a gun (took from his pocket).

Life in the Navy will draw him out (give him a chance to show his real character).

The car drew up outside our house (stopped).

The police drew up a list of suspects (made, complied).

i) Fall

The enemy fell back rapidly (retreated).

We've no butter—we'll have to fall back on margarine (resort to).

The roof of our house fell in yesterday (collapsed).

My eyes fell on a beautiful rose (I saw).

The sales have fallen off (declined).

She and her husband are always falling out (quarrelling).

I lost my money and all my plans fell through (came to nothing).

j) Get

Although she's very old, she gets about a lot (travels).

The book's on a high shelf and I can't get at it (reach).

The thieves got away through the window (escaped).

I've got behind with my work again (become late).

The train gets in at midnight (arrives).

Don't get off the bus till it stops (alight from).

He was accused of murder, but he got off (was acquitted).

I don't exactly how old she is, but I know she's getting on (advancing in age).

It's getting on for four o'clock now (approaching).

He can't get over the shock (recover from).

Can't you get round your father to give you the money (persuade)?

I tried to telephone you but couldn't get through (get connected).

He got through his examination (passed).

I can't get through all this work (finished).

We want to get up a party this week-end (organize).

k) Give

Don't give away any secrets (betray).

The bride's father gave her away (presented her ceremonially to the bridegroom).

The enemy tormented him, but he would not give in (surrender).

Our supply of petrol has given out (finished).

I have given up smoking (stopped, renounced).

She overworked and her health gave way (collapsed).

i) Go

Go along! You're treading on my feet (move forward)!

He has never yet gone back on his word (failed to keep his promise).

The days go by so quickly (pass).

This train goes by electricity (functions by means of).

That shop has gone down lately (deteriorated).

The prices never seem to go down (fall).

His speech went down very well (was received).

He went for the doctor (went to fetch).

He went for the burglar with a stick (attacked).

Shall we go for a walk, a drive, a run or a swim (go to have)?

They went into the whole matter of political secrecy (investigated).

He's going in for medicine (making his career in).

Another atom bomb went off yesterday (exploded).

This meat has gone off (lost its freshness).

The baby went off to sleep at once (fell asleep).

Please go on with your work (continue).

She goes on at him until he leaves the house (nags, talks angrily to him).

Put some coal on the fire it well go out (die. Used of light and heat).

The tide has gone out a long way (receded).

He can be relied on to go through with the work (complete).

He says he can't go without his tea (sacrifice, accept lack of).

m) Lay

She has some money laid by in case of emergency (put away).

Those soldiers laid down their arms (relinquished).

These soldiers laid down their lives for their country (sacrificed).

He keeps laying down the law to me about my wifely duties (formulating dogmatically).

The house is ready: the water is already laid on (connected).

We laid out a lot of money on the garden (spent).

He was laid out by a blow on the head (knocked unconscious).

They laid up a large store of coal (amassed).

She was laid up for weeks with influenza (confined to bed. Passive only).

n) Look

He was looking at the beautiful view (regarding; observing).

Her grandmother will look after the children (take care of).

They look down on us because we haven't got a car (despise).

She looked in just to see if we needed anything (visited in passing).

I'm looking for a new house (seeking).

Will you look into the matter of the lost books (examine)?

He looks on my parties with disgust (regards, views).

Look out! The saucepan is burning (be careful)!

His work is looking up now (improving).

They looked up to this great man (respected, admired).

She looked round and saw someone following her (looked behind).

o) Make

He made straight for the door (went towards).

She made one of his old shirts into a blouse (transformed).

The burglars made off quickly when the man appeared (went away).

That dog has made off with my shoe (carried away).

I don't know what do make of her (I can't understand her).

He made a lot on that deal (profited financially by).

Can you make out what this word means (understand).

The doctor made out the whole story up (invented, fabricated).

She makes up too heavily (uses cosmetics).

After a quarrel you must kiss and make up (be reconciled).

We need one more person to make up the four at bridge (complete).

The chemist made up the prescription (compounded the medicine).

Here's five rupees to make up for the one you lost (compensate for).

The secretary made up to her employer in order to get promotion (sought favour with).

p) Put

He put down the rebellion with a firm hand (suppressed).

Let me put your address down in my book (write).

I put in a lot of work on that article (did).

He is going to put in for a higher salary (apply for).

We must put off the picnic until next week (postpone).

The bad smell in that restaurant really puts me off (repels).

She puts on a very superior expression (assumes).

Put the light out before you go to bed (extinguish).

She seemed rather put out by letter (distressed, disconcerted, usually in passive only).

Will it put you out if we come today (inconvenience)?

Would you put me through to this number (connected by telephone)?

I'm sorry to put you to all this trouble (give, usually with words like trouble, inconvenience, expense).

They've put up the price of bread again (raised).

I can't put up with that terrible noise (endure).

His sister puts him up to a lot of mischief (incites).

q) Run

She ran away with an actor (eloped with).

These holidays do run away with the money (consume, take).

I ran across my niece yesterday (met by chance).

She looks very pale and run down (in poor health. passive only).

He's always running other people down (disparaging).

I ran into an old friend this morning (met suddenly).

My mother-in-law runs on so much (talks continuously).

She was run over by a car (overthrown).

Turn off the tap or the bathwater will run over (overflow).

He ran through all his money in a week (spent rapidly).

My wife runs up too many bills (accumulates).

I ran up against another old friend (met by chance. Like run into and run across).

r) See

I'll see about it later on (do it later. Polite refusal to act immediately).

My wife saw me off at the airport (saw my departure).

These people want to see over the house (visit and examine).

I can see through your flattery (I am not deceived by).

Will you see to the dinner (attend to, make arrangements for).

Please see to it that the potatoes are properly cooked (make sure that).

s) Set

The Court set aside the decree (annulled).

He soon set about organizing a school (began).

The rain has set in for the day, I think (become established).

He set his dogs on the burglar (encouraged them to attack).

I'm setting off for New York tomorrow (beginning a journey to).

Now set to work and build the house (begin).

His father set him up in a business of his own (established).

t) Speak

His behaviour at school speaks well for him (puts him a favourable light).

His brother is an art collector, but he himself has no painting to speak of (worth mentioning).

Don't be afraid to speak out (speak freely).

Speak up! I can't hear you (speak more loudly).

u) Stand

They were loyal and always stood by each other (supported).

Ltd. stands for "limited." (represents).

My uncle is standing for Parliament (is a candidate for election).

Don't be victims of tyranny! Stand up for your rights (maintain, defend)!

The boxer stood up to his opponent splendidly (faced, resisted).

v) Take

That boy takes after his father (resembles).

You are wrong: you must take back all you said (retract).

Please dictate it to me and I'll take it down now (write).

Do you take me for a fool (assume to be)?

The lecture was good but I couldn't take it all in (understand).

The thief's charming manners quite took me in (deceived me).

The aeroplane took off at six o' clock (left the ground).

He took over his father's business (acquired).

I took to that girl at once (was attracted to).

She's taken to eating far too much chocolate (formed habit of).

That table takes up too much room (occupies).

w) Throw

Politeness is thrown away on that man (wasted, not appreciated).

He threw himself into the task of digging the garden (engaged vigorously in it).

I've got a bad cold and I can't throw it off (lose, get rid of it).

His death threw open the door to my promotion (made possible).

The Government threw out the bill (rejected).

He proposed marriage to her and then threw her over for an actress (abandoned, deserted).

He then threw up his job in England and went to Canada (resigned, gave up).

x) Turn

My sister has suddenly turned against me (become hostile).

They turned down his application (refused).

We're going to turn in early tonight (go to bed).

That ugly girl turned into a beautiful woman (became).

My wife turned on me and called me a fool (attacked unexpectedly).

This factory turns out hundreds of cars a week (produces, manufactures).

The tea party turned out to be a great success (proved).

Her mother turned her out of the house (caused to leave).

In time of trouble, you can always turn to me (ask for help).

My uncle from Australia turned up yesterday (appeared unexpectedly).

y) Work

He works off his bad temper on his family (vents, gets rid of).

Try to work on him and persuade him (influence).

The pupil worked out the problem quickly (solved).

She always gets very worked up before examination (excited).

2. IDIOMS WITH CLOTHES

Those two men are hand in glove with each other (closely associated).

She is dressed up to the nines (overdressed, too elaborately dressed).

You will have to pull your socks up if you want to pass the examination (make a greater effort).

The children love dressing up (wearing fancy dress).

It is foolish to wash your dirty linen in public (air private grievances openly).

She looks serious but she is laughing up her sleeve (laughing secretly).

This man is very difficult: you must handle him with kid gloves (treat him very carefully).

This politician is a turncoat (someone who changes his opinions and deserts his principles).

She told me a good joke and I capped it with a better one (improved upon it).

He is tied to his mother's apron-strings (too dependent on his mother).

You are talking through your hat (talking nonsense).

My sister is a terrible bluestocking (a clever, learned woman used in a derogatory sense).

3. IDIOMS WITH PARTS OF THE BODY

I'll back you up in your suggestion (support you).

This is more than flesh and blood can stand (human nature)!

He shot the man in cold blood (deliberately).

She made a clean breast of the matter (confessed fully).

I always see eye to with my sister (agree with).

Keep an eye on my luggage, please (watch).

Don't trust him: he's two-faced (dishonest).

She let the opportunity slip through her fingers (lost the opportunity).

My fingers are all thumbs today, and I can't tie up this parcel (my hands are clumsy).

He has all the facts at his fingers' end (knows them thoroughly).

I just snap my fingers at his silly rules (show contempt for).

He turned a deaf ear to my request (disregarded).

In all the panic she did not turn a hair (remained calm).

I don't care for his very off-hand manner (too casual, lacking in respect).

Lend me a hand with this heavy case, please (help).

The two cars were involved in a head-on collision (direct).

She is head over heels in love (completely, madly).

He always loses his head in a crisis (panics).

This student is head and shoulders above the others (far superior to).

You can't teach him: he's too pig-headed (obstinate).

His brother tries hard to learn he's thick-headed (stupid).

Success went to his head (intoxicated him, made him vain).

Your cruelty broke my heart (made me despair).

She is a woman after my own heart (ideal).

Her sister always wears her heart on her sleeve (shows her feelings).

That boy looks very down at heel (badly dressed).

When the policeman came the children took to their heels (ran away).

We paid through the nose for this bread (paid too much).

She turns up her nose at this kind of house (despises).

I greeted her, but she gave me the cold shoulder (ignored me).

4. IDIOMS WITH ANIMALS

This boy is a silly ass (a foolish person).

She's got bats in the belfry (is mad).

His letter has a sting in the tail (unpleasant part at the end).

She and her husband lead a cat-and-dog life (a life of quarrels).

They're making a cat's paw of you (using you as a tool).

Now you've let the cat out of the bag (revealed a secret)!

I haven't seen you for donkey's years (a long time).

That man's a wolf in sheep's clothing (a hypocrite).

In London she's like a fish out of water (out of her element).

He's as clumsy as a bull in a china shop (harmful and out of place).

What a cock-and-bull story that was (incredibly silly)!

She shed crocodile tears over her brother's death (pretended sorrow).

The poor man leads a dog's life (a wretched, miserable life).

That big chair is an absolute white elephant (unwanted possession).

Your brother is a dark horse (has unexpected powers and may surprise us).

She's always fishing for compliments (trying to get).

Your father is a spoilsport—a real dog in the manger (one who will neither enjoy something himself nor let others enjoy it).